More
PARSHA
PARABLES

Stories and anecdotes that
shine a new light on the weekly
Torah portion & holidays

By Rabbi Mordechai Kamenetzky

BENTSH
PRESS

More Parsha Parables

ISBN: 0-9657697-1-2

Published by:
Bentsh Press
P.O. Box 224
Hewlett, NY 11557

Distributed by:
Feldheim Publishers
200 Airport Executive Park
Nanuet, NY 10954
(914) 356-2282

Designed and produced by:
Dynagrafik Design Studios
Cover by:
Spotlight Design

Printed and bound in the United States of America
by Noble Book Press

To order additional copies of this book,
please call (516) 374-7363 ext. 124
e-mail: rmk@torah.org

For all comments and suggestions,
please write:
Rabbi Mordechai Kamenetzky
P.O. Box 224
Hewlett, NY 11557
Fax: (516) 569-7954

People say that stories are told
to put children to sleep . . .

I say they are told to wake
the slumbering soul.

Rabbi Nachman of Breslov

THIS PUBLICATION HAS BEEN MADE POSSIBLE
THROUGH A GENEROUS GRANT FROM
KEREN MA'ASIM TOVIM

KEREN MA'ASIM TOVIM

Ours are changing times. More and more people endeavor not merely to keep up with the proverbial Joneses, but also with the Dow Jones. We live in an era of stock market fluctuations, ever- increasing choices of mutual funds and portfolio managers, and the need to diversify one's portfolio. How does one make an investment where the principal is secure, dividends are guaranteed for the future, and performance is not subject to vacillating economic indicators?

One of the most venerated teachers and revered *mussar* (ethics) guides of the 19th Century, and a noted student of the great Chasam Sofer, was the *Peleh Yoetz*, *zt"l*. In his widely acclaimed *sefer*, which covers all aspects of the Jew's relationship to Torah, the *Peleh Yoetz* answers our investment questions. "Consider, and you will find that almost no sizeable amount of money measures up to the greatness of this *mitzvah* (helping in the publication of a *sefer*), for every expenditure on a *mitzvah* is for its time. One performs the *mitzvah* and completes the task. However, the one who gives towards the publication of a *sefer*, his righteousness lasts forever, for generation after generation. Furthermore, his deed benefits multitudes, and their merits are all credited to him.

"This noble deed will lead him, and will follow him. Praised is he! Oh, how wonderful is his share! He invested in a good name, he invested in words of Torah, he invested in life in *Olam Haba*, and dividends will pour forth even in the ephemeral world." Through the publication of *seforim*, Torah becomes even greater, by being disseminated to the world. Therefore, the *Peleh Yoetz* advises, it is proper for those who are able to give generously, and by doing so, *chelek k'chelek yochlu im ha'chochom*, they will share and share alike with the *chochom*, the author.

The well known story of Shmuel HaNagid, the 11th-century scribe and treasurer in the court of the King of Spain, is quite apropos. Shmuel achieved a very high post in the King's cabinet, which aroused the wrath of anti-Semitic Moslem clerics. When they leveled charges of embezzlement against Shmuel, the King, feeling obligated to investigate the charges, summoned Shmuel and asked him to submit a detailed list of his assets. When Shmuel provided it, the King agreed with the clerics, that Shmuel's listing was too paltry and therefore patently false. Since Shmuel was certainly concealing his embezzlement, the King promptly ordered the confiscation of Shmuel's assets and his incarceration.

Some time later, as the King was trying to come to terms with the absence of his most brilliant adviser, he decided to visit Shmuel in his cell and demand an explanation for Shmuel's assumed betrayal. After greeting the King, Shmuel explained that his list represented monies given to various charities. "The merits for those deeds, no one can take away from me," Shmuel said. "They are mine forever! Those are my real assets! The assets in my possession? That's another matter. Those can be mine today and confiscated tomorrow! So how can I count them as truly mine?"

The instructive lesson is clear: the value of assets, like the Dow Jones, can fluctuate, oscillate, or even evaporate. But an act of giving—a *zikuy harabim*, one that benefits multitudes, in which the *mitzvah* of learning Torah is a direct consequence of one's act of giving—that act, that asset, that investment, that righteousness is forever his, *l'dor dor*, from generation to generation.

The publication of *More Parsha Parables* is a project completed with the help of *Keren Ma'asim Tovim*, the sole purpose being the dissemination of these warm, touching, enjoyable homilies, a new perspective on age-old themes, to multitudes thirsty for God's words. Untold lives and Shabbos tables have been enriched and enhanced by the original essays that were culled in this book, presented as weekly FaxHomilies and *drasha* e-mails, easily accessible to all people each according to their own level of insight.

Keren Ma'asim Tovim offers its deepest gratitude to the author, Rabbi Mordechai Kamenetzky, for his creative approach to *parsha* analysis, and for allowing this foundation to share in his noble endeavor. And creativity is the heart of the project! For as Shlomo *HaMelech* says in *Shir HaShirim*, "*samchuni ba'ashishos, rapdooni ba'tapuchim*" (support me with wine bottles, comfort me with apples). The Gemara adds, *ashishos*, wine bottles, refer to *halacha* (Jewish law), and *tapuchim*, apples, refer to *agadah* (homiletic passages).

The question is self-evident: why is *halacha* symbolized by wine and *agadah* by apples? Rabbi Boruch Epstein, *zt"l*, the author of the Torah Temimah, interprets the *posuk* in a fascinating manner. Our sages teach us a key difference between *halacha* and *agadah*: if one finds a *halachic* ruling written by a scholar from centuries ago, it is deemed more reliable than if a contemporary *posek* wrote it. The more ancient the author, the more his ruling will be accepted and favored. The simile to wine—the older the better – applies to *halacha*. In contrast, *agadah* is interpreted and expounded in the spirit of the times. Generally, agadic exegesis is based on the status of the audience, its position in life. The more the homily lecture is up-to-date, compatible with current events and new challenges in life, the more it is pleasing, relevant and effective. The simile for *agadah* is the apple — the newer, the fresher, the better!

Rabbi Kamenetzky's insights on each *parsha*, his masterful blending of anecdotes and secular adages into Torah morals, may be the most innovative "*rapdooni ba'tapuchim*" yet. "*Ki cholas ahava ani*," the *posuk* continues. We yearn and crave for these sweet and lovely *tapuchim, mi'day Shabbat b'Shabbato*.

On behalf of *Keren Ma'asim Tovim*, I dedicate the publication of *More Parsha Parables* to my pride and joy, my children, Heshy and Pia, Zevy and Rivky, Motty, Shloimie, and Leah Brocha. By dedicating this *sefer* to them, my aim is to insure that the values and ideals so eloquently presented here, and symbolized by our assistance in its publication, are transmitted to my children.

May it be His will that I continue to *shep* loads of *nachas* from them as we witness the glorious chain of our heritage as it endures forever.

Avrohom Pinchos Berkowitz
Keren Ma'asim Tovim

ישראל בן זכריה לייב ע"ה
and
טובה מריאשא בת חיים ע"ה

IRVING & MARCELLA BIRNBAUM

of blessed memory

Irving was a master storyteller who applied charm, wit, and love for his Jewish heritage throughout his illustrious career as a businessman and caterer.

Marcella's beautiful handicrafts and artistic creations revealed her deep connection with spirituality. Her dedication to helping the very young and very old influenced the lives of her family who revere her commitment to *chesed*.

Their love for *Yiddishkeit* and a *Yiddisheh Mai'seh* will live on as an inspiration to all of us.

Howard Birnbaum & Family
Leonard Birnbaum & Family

A special ישר כח to Norman Septimus & Eli Mendlowitz
As Shadchanim par excellence, you have helped me fulfill the dictum
עשה לך רב וקנה לך חבר

Howard

RABBI BENJAMIN KAMENETZKY
357 BARNARD AVENUE • WOODMERE, N. Y. 11598

ב"ה

תשרי ד', תשנ"ט

To My Dear Son ר' מרדכי שליט"א,

When you published *Parsha Parables* I expressed my heartfelt congratulations and my very best wishes on what was surely an auspicious occasion — for you and our family. For I watched with amazement the impact that these gems of Torah thoughts have made upon thousands of readers across the globe who have come closer to Hashem and to our Torah through your efforts.

Now, with the publication of *More Parsha Parables*, I once again feel a profound sense of pride and gratitude, that not only the legacy of Torah, but the legacy of my sainted and revered father, z"tl, is being preserved and passed down to new generations thirsting eagerly for genuine Torah teachings.

It is that Mesorah which binds the People of Israel — and insures the unbroken chain of the mesorah, the transmittal of Torah knowledge from one generation to the next.

As my beloved son has done magnificent work here on Long Island, so may he merit a long life of teaching Torah to the world.

With love and affection,
Your father

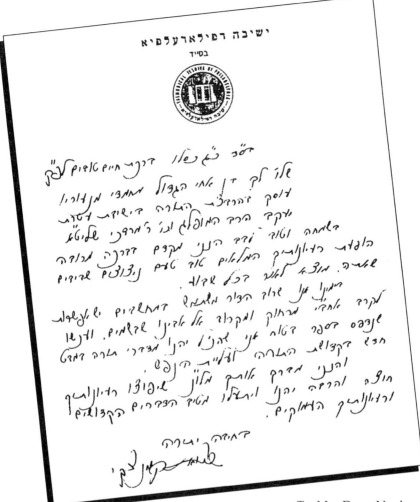

To My Dear Nephew,
Rabbi Mordechai Kamenetzky, whom I have loved since his youth, who spreads Torah at Yeshiva Ateres Yaakov. It is with a joyous heart that I greet you with blessings on the printing of your weekly Torah thoughts that are filled with sparks of insight.

I am sure that when a majority of a generation uses computers, there is an increased ability to touch the hearts of our brethren from far and near and bring them to their Father in Heaven. Now that these Torah thoughts will be printed in a book, I am sure that many more people will enjoy the *Divrei Torah* with a new look into the sanctity of Torah and the elevation of the soul.

I therefore bless you with my heart and soul to spread your ideas forward, that people may enjoy, grow and be inspired from the beautiful thoughts and words.

Affectionately,

Rabbi Shmuel Kamenetsky

Rabbi Yacov Lipschutz
P.O. Box 178
Monsey, New York 10952

Tishrei 5759

In Rabbi Mordechai Kamenetzky's first work, *Parsha Parables*, he offered his reader profound insights into each parsha of the week. Now, in this worthy successor volume, *More Parsha Parables*, he has once again gleaned from his vast storehouse of Torah knowledge clear and uplifting messages, giving broader and deeper meaning to the Torah words we so revere.

Indeed, Rabbi Kamenetzky's unique ability to accompany each message with a moral tale of great Tzadikim and Torah leaders brings to life the inspiring words of the *parshiyot*. There is no doubt that reading this wonderful sefer, and sharing its wit and wisdom with the entire family at the Shabbos table, will add to the beauty of every Shabbos and Yom Tov.

Sincerely,

Rabbi Yacov Lipschutz

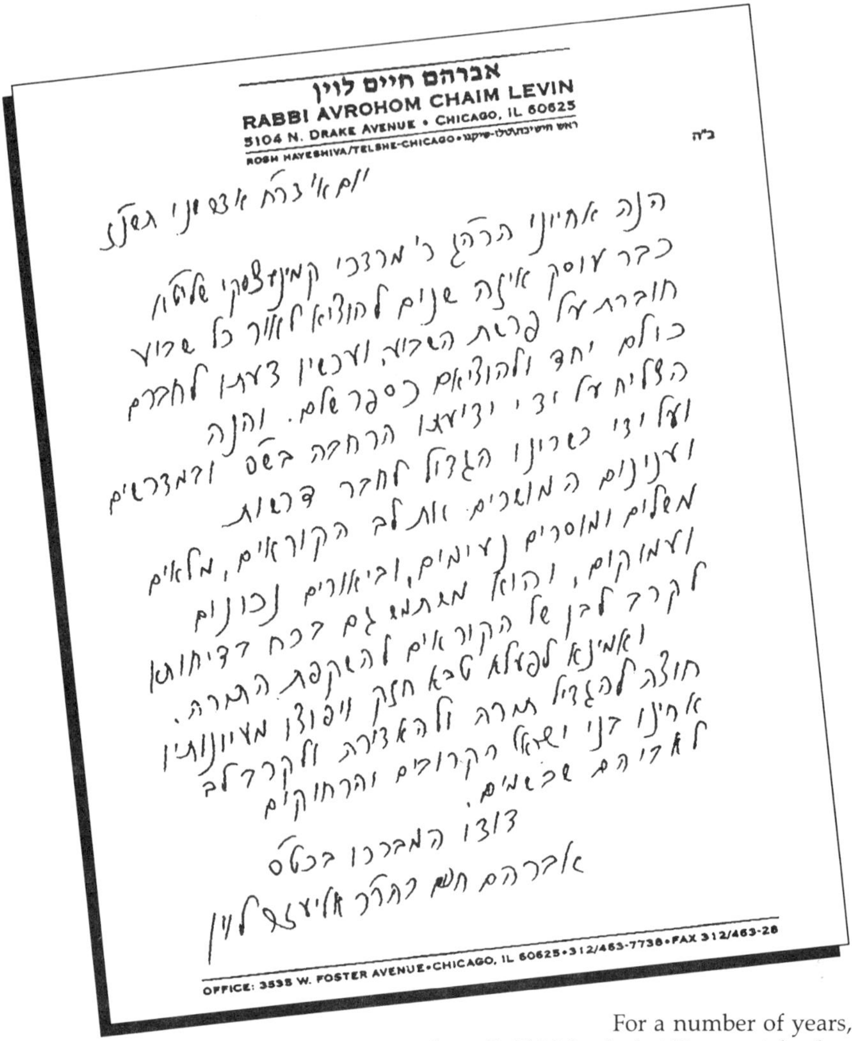

אברהם חיים לוין
RABBI AVROHOM CHAIM LEVIN
5104 N. DRAKE AVENUE • CHICAGO, IL 60625
ROSH HAYESHIVA/TELSHE-CHICAGO • ראש הישיבה/טעלז-שיקאגו

ב"ה

[Handwritten letter in Hebrew]

OFFICE: 3535 W. FOSTER AVENUE • CHICAGO, IL 60625 • 312/463-7738 • FAX 312/463-28

For a number of years, my nephew Rabbi Mordechai Kamenetzky, has been publishing weekly Torah thoughts on the *parsha*. Now, he has decided to collect and publish them in book form.

Through his vast knowledge of *Shas* and *Medrash* and because of his ability to compose *Drashot*, he has successfully written a book filled with insights and ideas including many parables, applicable Mussar, and accurate interpretations. He also uses a sense of humor to bring the reader closer to Torah *hashkafah* (outlook).

I am pleased to commend such a wonderful work, and say *Chazak*!

May your works enjoy widespread dissemination and enhance and expand the Torah learning of our brethren, both near and far, and draw their hearts closer to our Father in Heaven.

With warm greetings and Torah blessings,

Rabbi Avrohom Chaim Levin

Table of Contents

Foreword

Rabbi Dr. Abraham J. Twerski

Speaking of the Torah, the Talmud says, "Review it again and again, for everything is therein" *(Ethics of the Fathers 5:25)*. The Talmud is referring not only to the five books of Moses and the prophets, but also to the extended Torah, which includes all the commentaries and elaborations by Torah scholars throughout the ages. Torah also includes the anecdotes about our great Torah personalities, because it is their behavior that helps us implement the teachings of Torah and translate them into action.

While the volume of existing Torah literature is indeed great, there is never any closure to it, because being the wisdom of God, Torah is as infinite as God Himself. Every generation can add to the treasury of Torah knowledge.

Rabbi Mordechai Kamenetzky has not only enriched our Torah literature, but has also brought it into many households in digestible portions. His weekly messages on the insights of the Torah portion for the week have become the focus of discussions at many Shabbos tables, enabling parents and children to share in Torah wisdom.

We live in an age of unprecedented scientific and technological advances. But while science and technology can provide us with more comfortable ways to live, they can say nothing about the ultimate purpose of life itself. None of the comforts and conveniences we have reaped from science have given meaning to life, and they cannot fill the vacancy resulting from a sense of purposelessness. For life to have meaning, we must turn to Torah, the textbook of life provided by the Creator of life.

The rich insights in *More Parsha Parables*, presented by Rabbi Kamenetzky, can serve as a beacon of light that can help us discover the true values which can make every individual's life purposeful and meaningful, and thereby lead to a pathway of happiness.

Introduction

It is exciting to publish a book; it is even more exciting to publish a second one. As the impact of FaxHomily, the weekly Torah facsimile, and its e-mail edition, broadened, I realized that the message was becoming greater than its medium. The collection of bits and bytes, fax paper and stapled fax sheets, needed greater permanence. *Parsha Parables* was a fast sell-out, as requests poured in from the cyber-impaired, the computerless, and the fax-disabled. And thus, *More Parsha Parables*.

Throughout this volume, I have tried to keep the format the exact style as the first book, with but a few minor differences. Always looking for a Jewish anecdote, and occasionally a secular one from which I would be able to derive a moral lesson that has inherent Torah value, I sometimes peruse various anecdotal and historical anthologies. A few months before I began editing *More Parsha Parables*, I noticed that many spell the names of our Patriarchs and Biblical leaders as they are pronounced in Hebrew. Moses is Moshe and Abraham is Avraham. Some of those volumes are *New York Times* bestsellers and even though the names of the key players were not anglicized, the readers and reviewers understood who the protagonists were.

I took a cue, and even though *More Parsha Parables* is meant for a wide spectrum of readers, including the most secular, I felt it proper to retain Hebrew names and many words in their original form. It reminded me of something that happened in the Five Towns of Long Island, back in 1970.

My uncle, who was a *kollel* scholar in Lakewood, New Jersey and scion of a *chassidic* dynasty, moved to Cedarhurst, Long Island. He opened a small *chassidic shteeble* in which he served as the Rebbe. Our town was accustomed to fine rabbis who were polished speakers and orated in the vernacular of the typical pulpit rabbi of the late 1950s. Their style was elegant and it showed — especially when they referred to our Creator in their speeches as "the Lord, our God" and "the Almighty."

The first week that my uncle spoke in his synagogue, he left "our Lord" on Park Avenue. In His stead the *Ribbono Shel Olam*, the yeshivah expression for Master of the Universe, moved in. Thank God, I mean thank the *Ribbono Shel Olam*, He has remained a fixture in this community ever since.

In this volume, I feel comfortable calling our Patriarchs and leaders by their original names. Perhaps the names Moshe *Rabbeinu* and Yaakov *Avinu* and Shlomo *HaMelech* will one day replace Moses, Jacob, and King Solomon in the vernacular.

And in that vein, I thank the *Ribbono Shel Olam* for all He has provided me in publishing this book as well as in every aspect of my life.

Who's on First?

Ensuring that the names are written correctly is one task, but getting the players right in the story is sometimes a bit more arduous. Often the impact of a tale eclipses the individual protagonist, and through the words of the speakers and the ears of the listeners, one Lithuanian *Rosh Yeshiva's* experience turns into a *Chassidic* Rebbe's adventure. This has occurred to the extent that I was shocked to pick up a book and see a story that I had always heard attributed to a great rabbi told about a football player!

Years ago, I heard a story about Rabbi Yecheskel Abramsky, the *Av Beis Din* (chief rabbinical judge) of the London Beth Din, who was called to testify in civil court about the character and nature of a man involved in a suit. After the rabbi affirmed to tell the truth, the attorney asked a few preliminary questions.

"Is it true, Rabbi Abramsky," the attorney asked, "that you are proficient in Jewish literature?"

Rabbi Abramsky answered, "Yes."

"How proficient?"

"I have mastered the entire Talmud and Bible, Midrash and related codes."

"Is it true, Rabbi Abramsky," the attorney asked, "that you are a leading authority in Jewish Law?"

Again the rabbi answered in the affirmative.

"And what is your ranking?"

The rabbi solemnly stated that he was the leading religious authority in England and in fact, perhaps on the entire European continent.

At this juncture the judge could no longer contain himself.

"Isn't there room for humility in your religion?" he asked.

"Of course there is, Your Honor," came the soft reply, "but I'm under oath."

The only disheartening epilogue is that several months ago,

among my secular perusals, was a book entitled *Chicken Soup for the Soul*. Among the stories was one about Frank Szymanski, a center for the Notre Dame football team back in the 1940s. Szymanski was once called as a witness in a civil suit in South Bend, Indiana.

During his testimony the judge asked him about his athletic abilities. The normally unassuming and low-keyed Szymanski answered that he was the best center in the history of the Notre Dame football program.

When asked by his coach about his uncharacteristic lack of humility, the player answered that despite his misgivings about bragging, he had no choice. After all, he was under oath.

Most recently I was shown the same story about noted physicist, Henry Augustus Rowland, in an anthology by Isaac Asimov.

While I am now confused about which came first — the great *tzadik*, the scientist, or the athlete — I know that one must take many stories, with the proverbial grain of salt, unless, of course, the storyteller is under oath!

Stories, in general, sometimes take on a life of their own. Occasionally the heroes adopt new identities, sometimes amazing peripherals attach themselves to the plot and sometimes they are figments of the storyteller's imagination. Yet, I love to use them, realizing that I put faith in the adage that the person who believes that *all* the amazing stories about the great rabbis are true is a fool, while he who believes that *none* are true is an *apikores* (heretic)!

Finding stories I have read about *tzadikim* people (righteous) attributed in secular tomes to laymen made me feel a little more comfortable about using secular anecdotes and *bubba maasehs* in this volume. Some are about professionals, still others about politicians. At first, I was reluctant to use stories about politicians, and surely rogues and charlatans as parables to learn a Torah lesson, and then I read about Reb Moshe Leib, the Rebbe of Sasov.

Reb Moshe Leib once stopped by a tavern and overheard a conversation between two drunk peasants.

"Boris," cried one to his friend, "I love you!"

"Liar!" the other drunken peasant shouted with vehemence.

"Why do you call me a liar? Boris, I truly love you with all my heart!"

Boris responded, "I will prove you do not love me. If you love me tell me where I am hurting. If you know where it hurts me, if you know what I am missing, *then* you can shout that you love me."

Reb Moshe Leib taught this message, learned from a drunken peasant, to his *chassidim*.

"One can not say he loves his friend unless he knows where he is hurting."

With apologies to my friends in the House and Senate, if the holy Reb Moshe Leib of Sassov can learn from a drunken peasant, then this simple Reb Mordechai can learn from a politician!

Of course, the lessons learned from *Gedolei Yisroel* (Torah sages) transcend any that can be learned from those who are all too well steeped in the material pursuits of this world.

At a lecture I gave at the Agudas Yisrael of Long Island I mentioned that there are two adages in *Chazal* (Talmudic literature) that seem somewhat contradictory.

The *Tana D'bei Eliyahu* tells us that *derech eretz kadmah l' Torah*, that decency and good character precede Torah scholarship, yet the *Mishna* in *Pirkei Avos* (*Ethics of our Fathers*, Chapter 3:17) tells us that if there is no Torah there is no *derech eretz*.

How is it possible, then, ever to attain either Torah or *derech eretz*? After all, if you can not attain either *derech eretz* without Torah or Torah without *derech eretz* then you can never attain either!

I saw a fascinating answer in the *Medrash Shmuel* on *Pirkei Avos*. He explains that there are two levels of *derech eretz*. One is common courtesy and *mentchlichkeit* — and they are a prerequisite to any level of Torah acquisition. That level of *derech eretz* is expected and required from everyone, even those who have no Torah knowledge. However, there is a higher level of *derech eretz*, one that is only attained after intense Torah study — that *high* degree of *derech eretz* and concern for others is unattainable without Torah.

This differentiation of two levels of *derech eretz* brought to mind two stories with similar themes, but with a completely different cast, illustrating *derech eretz* on two vastly different levels. The first is a humanistic level of *derech eretz*, the second a Torah level of *derech eretz*.

The first story occurred with Abraham Lincoln, and I used it to illustrate a point in *Parshas Vayechi*.

At noon on January 1st, 1863, the final draft of the Emancipation Proclamation was placed in front of Abraham Lincoln. He stared intensely at it as it lay before him on his desk.

He picked up his pen to sign the document, and was about to dip the quill into the ink when he hesitated and put his arm down. He paused, closed his eyes, and began the process again. Determinedly, he picked up the quill, dipped it in the ink, and put it down. With a grim face he turned to Secretary of State William N. Seward and said, "My hands have been shaking since nine o'clock this morning. My right hand is almost paralyzed. If I am ever to go down in history, it will be for this act. My whole self is in it. However, if my hand trembles when I sign this proclamation, whoever examines it will say hereafter, 'he hesitated.'"

With that, the President composed himself, dipped the quill into the ink, and slowly but resolutely signed in perfect form — Abraham Lincoln.

The other story is about my grandfather. After his stroke in 1984, my grandfather, HaGaon Rabbi Yaakov Kamenetzky, of blessed memory, lived with his daughter Rebbitzen Rivka and Reb Hirsch Diskind in Baltimore. In addition to their loving and devoted care, students would come to help my grandfather with his daily needs.

One of the boys asked my grandfather to autograph his copy of *Emes L'Yaakov*, a *sefer* (Torah book) my grandfather had recently authored. The boy brought the book to Reb Yaakov and left it on the table. A few days later, my grandfather returned it to him — with the name signed neatly in Hebrew letters, Yaakov Kamenetzky.

It was not until later that my aunt and uncle found a piece of paper folded neatly with the name Yaakov Kamenetzky written over and over — at least twenty times — until it was immaculately written by a man who had lost movement in his hand. Only then did he sign the book. He, too, did not want the young boy to think — even for a moment — he had hesitated.

And then I understood the answer of the *Medrash Shmuel*. President Lincoln had great *derech eretz*. Historians and countrymen should never think he hesitated when signing the Emancipation Proclamation. Reb Yaakov was also worried. He worried about the young student who might have thought he hesitated. That is the *derech eretz* that comes after Torah scholarship.

What's on Second

People often ask me how I come up with a story each week that clarifies a point in the portion. Honestly, it is not easy! As the pressure to find little stories that fit each *parsha* increased, I, together with my family began to look at the world as a great parable. My children would remark on mundane incidents that occurred in the supermarket check-out line or while greeting toll booth clerks on the highway, as potential fodder for my weekly fax. They are. Almost every incident in life helps one realize that there is more to life than what meets the eye. But the challenge is how to relate it to each week's *parsha*.

British biologist Charles Darwin, a man whose opinion of his forebears is, obviously, antithetical to the opinion I have of mine, spent eight years of his life studying barnacles. Over the years he amassed a collection of no fewer than 10,000 barnacles stored in various rooms in his home.

Once, his son visited a friend, and, like children often do, roamed through the various rooms of the home. But he was bewildered and asked his friend, "Where does your dad keep his barnacles?"

We all have our barnacles. They are the little things we study to increase our knowledge, understanding, and even pleasure. Some study the fluctuations of the market, others the latest gizmos and gadgets, still others the statistics of ball players. But the barnacles should lend a greater purpose. They should make us better people somehow — in some way. Otherwise they are only sea urchins.

Though in no way do I consider all those who have helped in the publication of this book as tiny barnacles, appreciation for their help is mindfully stored in the display case of my heart.

First and foremost, I thank my wife Sora for being a pillar of support as I write the weekly *D'var Torah* and while I prepared this volume for publication.

She knows that when she relates to me the episodes of the daily occurrences of caring for and nurturing our family, I may be thinking, "How can I use that episode in the supermarket for next week's fax?" There is no parable for her devotion.

Many people were involved in producing this book and I'd like to thank all of them. Others, afraid to leave out anyone, just give a blanket thank you. Without a blanket, I'll try to cover everyone.

Once again my editor, Abby Mendelson, has done a superb job in clarifying my ideas with his sharp revisions and corrections while still pleasing the good people at Strunk and White. Despite a busy schedule and authoring a recent book about the Pittsburgh Steelers, he finds the time to look over the weekly fax and make corrections. This volume is influenced by his expertise in grammar, grace, and style.

For the same person — who portrays the fierce gruffness of the Jack Lamberts and the meanness of the Joe Greenes of this world in his other works — to be able to help develop and illustrate the refined sensitivities and impeccable civility of *Gedolei Yisrael* in *this* volume takes true talent. *Yasher Koach.*

Ethel Gottlieb, has fine-tuned the book like one who has all the musical notes in hand then carefully and meticulously ensures that all the instruments are in sync for the symphony. Her attention to detail is remarkable, and I thank her down to the last period.

Paula Tausch helped in retyping corrections in addition to helping administrate the nearly 1000 subscribers to the weekly Torah facsimile, Fax-Homily.

Steve Kollander, a dentist by trade, helps me by perusing the *parsha parables* before they are faxed and e-mailed worldwide; his comments and corrections are *always* appreciated and *sometimes* even listened to!

Yitzchok Feldheim, of Feldheim publishers, did a wonderful job distributing *Parsha Parables*. Within a year of publication they were sold out! I am sure, with the help of Hashem, he will be as efficient with this volume!

Neil Rosen was gracious enough to warehouse the 1000 volumes that I saved for our Yeshiva's distribution. Though he warehouses literally thousands of all sorts of barnacles, he cared for my books with exceptional devotion and was always available to open the warehouse for me. In addition, he has helped guide my prose to a level that could be appreciated by a secular audience as well as a religious one.

Rabbi Yitzchok Wolpin was gracious enough to review this work to help ensure a level of Torah sensitivity.

Once again, Phil Weinreich, of Noble Book Press, has produced a beautifully bound masterpiece. I thank him for his care and concern.

Dena Peker, of Dynagrafik, has done an excellent job of typesetting this manuscript. Gershon Eichorn's creative mind reflects amazingly in his beautiful cover.

I also want to thank Elle Fertig and the wonderful people at Ideas Inc. for their input.

I Don't Know's on Third

Though those who supply the material and monetary support are the essential builders of any physical body, the soul comes from moral support.

I must take this opportunity to thank those who fax and e-mail me with complimentary messages. I don't know who they are. Many of them do not sign their name and I haven't the time to translate fax numbers or e-mail addresses into human beings. But anonymous as they may want to be, they are a source of e-inspiration for yesterday's and tomorrow's messages. They offer encouragement and advice sometimes proposing new questions, stories, opinions, and insights. I am grateful for their warm wishes and good will.

On the back of the book jacket, I selected a sampling of some of the wonderful letters I have received over the years.

I thank Rabbi Yaakov Menken of Project Genesis for maintaining and expanding the e-mail list and his expeditious delivery of the e-mailed Torah to the thousands of subscribers whose only commonality is the "@" in their return address.

Pitchers

It would be wrong to leave out my friends and family members who often call me, to say, "I have a *gevaldikeh* story for you," or "I have a great *vort* for you." They have offered wonderful pitches to swing at.

My parents continue to be my best sales people. They are truly great pitchers!

My father, the Rosh Yeshiva of Yeshiva Toras Chaim of South Shore, is a constant source of Torah messages, stories and wisdom. He also presents the book to anybody who shows either an interest in *Yiddishkeit* or in supporting the Yeshiva of South Shore. Amazingly enough, those efforts have produced wonderful results on both ends!

My mother always compliments me on the stories, even

though she has heard them many times before they reach the fax. Most likely she is the source for many of them and I cherish her enthusiasm.

My father-in-law, Rabbi Yacov Lipschutz has been a wonderful source of insight and wisdom. May he and his Rebbitzen share only *nachas* and *simcha*.

My brother, Reb Zvi notifies me first of any late-breaking story that I may not yet have heard. Of course, they may have occurred in the 1700s, but if I have not yet heard it, consider it late-breaking.

My three brothers-in-law who live in Woodmere, Rabbi Yitzchok Knobel, Rabbi Simcha Lefkowitz, and Rabbi Shlomo Wilhelm are a constant source of guidance along with their wives, my sisters.

On my wife's side, my brother-in-law, Rabbi Pinchos Lipschutz, editor and publisher of *Yated Neeman* has been a source of advice and guidance. He has lent his professional expertise in every aspect of this work.

The wonderful Rabbeim, of Yeshiva of South Shore are always available for insightful input. I thank them all.

The (Heavy) Hitters

Last year my wife and I spent a *Shabbos* at the Homowack Hotel in the Catskill Mountains. After Shabbos, Abe Berkowitz, a man who has a distinct *chassidic* background and demeanor purchased a copy of *Parsha Parables*. I looked at him and thought of the stories of Max and Irving, and the tales of Detroit mobsters contained within, and apologetically said, "I'm not sure if this is your type of *sefer*," but he shrugged off my comment and bought a copy.

A few months later, I received a phone call from Mr. Berkowitz. He asked me to stop by his office, he told me how much he enjoyed the first volume and graciously offered to help publish a second. I am enormously grateful for his advice, encouragement and support that he has given throughout the entire process.

Richard Hirsch continues to be a major supporter of *FaxHomily*. It is through his encouragement, and that of the Henry and Myrtle Hirsch Foundation, that the weekly Torah message, and its faxed counterpart, *FaxHomily* has a combined weekly subscription roster of nearly 10,000 individuals. Each subscription is only sent upon request and is not spammed (something a kosher newsletter should never be) or junk faxed to anyone.

My good friend Howard Birnbaum has been a source of moral and financial support for the past three years. His encouragement helped turn the fax into books. I am enormously grateful for his friendship. May Hashem bless him and his family with the horn of plenty.

The Announcers

I would like to thank the authors and lecturers whose stories have impacted the lives of thousands of Jews world over. I have read their works, heard many of their lectures and have incorporated some of that knowledge in this volume. They include, Rabbi Paysach Krohn, author of the *Maggid* Series by Mesorah Publications. He has been available to help me whittle a two-page story into one paragraph by pointing out the most pertinent facts and nuances. Hanoch Teller's masterful volumes have also been a wonderful source of stories as well as many smiles.

Rabbi Dr. Abraham Yehoshua Twerski's stories, speeches, and volumes have been an inspiration to thousands and I am proud to count myself amongst them. Once again I would like to thank him for gracing this volume with a beautiful foreword.

The Talmud tells us that whoever repeats a Torah thought in the name of its author brings redemption to the world. It became a little more important to me after receiving an e-mail message from South Africa about a rabbi who had been using my weekly e-mail *drasha* as his weekly sermon — verbatim. The congregant printed his edition of the *Faxhomily-Drasha* and secretly distributed it to all the members of the congregation. They in turn began to read the sermon together with the rabbi — word by word. The rabbi has now found other sources for material.

I hope I do not make that omission. To that end, on the last page of this volume, I list the various books, both secular and religious whence I culled the stories used as parables in this volume.

We're Out!

I would like to close with a story that I heard from Rabbi Yaakov Horowitz, the Bostoner Rebbe of Lawrence, NY.

The Ponovezer Rav, Rabbi Yosef Kahaneman, of blessed memory, was one of the foremost builders of Torah in the post-war era. He was also a remarkable fund-raiser. Once he was welcomed into the home of a wealthy individual who was more interested in discussing Torah with him than giving money to the Ponovezer Yeshiva. Every time the Rav would begin to discuss the yeshiva's needs and begin asking the man to donate money for the construction of the new building, the man would begin to expound on a different Torah topic. Finally, Rav Kahaneman told him the following story:

A woman in Poland had a daughter who was past her prime. The matchmaker suggested that she alter her passport and claim she was much younger than her true age. He explained that he knew a Polish passport official who, for the right price, could make her any age she would like.

The official met the woman and then looked at the girl. "Oh, this is not a major problem. I am sure that there must have been an error in processing the original document. Of course, we can rectify this most egregious error. In fact, for a small service fee of 500 zloty I can take seven years off the date on her birth certificate, and we can have her at 21 years old!"

Despite the steep service charge, the mother heartily agreed and quickly took the money from her purse. Sensing that there were many more zloty in addition to the first 500, the officer held up his hand. "You know what," he smiled devilishly, "maybe there was a bigger error than we really had thought! Actually, for 700 zloty I could make her 20 years old!"

Reluctantly, the mother agreed and went to her purse for more zloty. At that point, the officer began to get quite greedy. "You know," he said, "for an additional 300 zloty I could even make her 18!"

The mother became very nervous. Quickly she handed over the 700 zloty and yelled, "No, thank you. Twenty years old is fine!" She grabbed her daughter. "Quick," she shouted, "let's get out of here! Soon we will be left with no more zloty and no more years!"

The Rav's message struck its mark. The man stopped his Torah-filled filibuster and handed over a sizable check.

I guess I've been on this introduction too long. I don't want to leave without Torah and without readers! Enjoy the book!

Mordechai Kamenetzky
Woodmere, NY
Kislev 5759

ספר בראשית

The Book of
Genesis

PARSHAS BRAISHIS

✎ *Eve of Life*

*D*oom, despair, and destruction: they all happened so quickly after the promise of an idyllic life. And all because of two bites of defiance — eating the forbidden fruit! Man, who was promised eternal bliss in the Garden of Eden, was now cursed with a plethora of misfortunes. He now would have to toil by the sweat of his brow, working an earth that produced thorn and thistle. His wife would now bear the pain of childbirth with all of its difficult physiological implications. In addition, these maledictions were crowned with the most powerful one of all, that "you are of dust and to dust you shall return" (*Genesis* 3:19).

But it seems that Adam viewed the news in proper perspective. In the verse that immediately follows the curses, Adam did not cast blame or lament his fate. He continued developing civilization exactly where he had left off. Prior to being coaxed by Eve to partake of the forbidden fruit, Adam had begun classifying all living things with names that appropriately described their attributes. And immediately after he was cursed, he continued. He named his wife.

"Adam called his wife Chava because she was the mother of all life" (*Genesis* 3:20).

Isn't it unsuitable for Adam to name his wife Chava — the mother of all life — immediately following the curse of death? What message is the Torah sending us with this juxtaposition?

※

Rabbi Levi Yitzchok of Berditchev was known for his love and good will toward his fellow Jews. He always tried to assess the good in people rather than expose the bad.

Once, on the Fast of *Tishah B'Av*, he saw a Jew eating in a non-kosher restaurant. Tapping lightly on the window of the establishment, Reb Levi Yitzchok summoned the man outside.

"Perhaps you forgot that today is a fast day?" Reb Levi Yitzchok queried.

"No, Rebbe," the man replied.

"Then perhaps you did not realize that this restaurant is not kosher," Reb Levi Yitzchok continued.

"No, Rebbe, I know it is a *traife* (non-kosher) eatery."

Though the admonition and ethical discourse that Reb Levi Yitzchok afforded the man is not recorded, legend has it that Reb Levi Yitzchok did try to find one saving grace for the dismal situation. He turned from the man, looked heavenward and quietly cried, "*Ribbono Shel Olam* (Master of the Universe) look at how wonderful Your children are. They may be eating on a fast day – even in a non-kosher restaurant, yet they refuse to utter a falsehood from their lips!"

❧

Adam heard the curse bestowed upon himself, his wife, and humanity for eternity. His immediate reaction was not scorn or criticism. Instead he named his wife Chava, derived from the word life. He viewed with a different perspective the woman whom he had once blamed for his downfall. He did not see in her the dawn of doom, but rather he saw the eve of life — and thus named her so.

After tragedy and defeat there is usually enough blame to share and spread. That, however, is not what Adam did. In a profoundly human act, he picked up the pieces and cherished the beauty of what was left.

Adam did not see this misfortune as the eve of destruction. Rather he saw himself standing at the side of the woman who would give life to the entire future of civilization. And he appreciated that life dearly.

PARSHAS NOACH

⟫ Tire of Babel

*T*he Flood was history. The era of robbery, greed, and corruption was washed away by its powerful waves. Peace and tranquility reigned. The entire world was now united — against the Almighty.

The world community decided that in the interest of harmony they would join forces and build a colossal tower to reach to the heavens. Then they would ascend the tower and do battle with God Himself.

It was an ambitious dream, but they were united and determined.

Hashem, however, had other plans. The *Midrash* tells us that He convened the same tribunal He had consulted with when creating man, and this time decided that He would not destroy the builders. Instead, He confused them: He changed their languages so they were not able to communicate. A man asked for a hammer and received a nail, a saw, or a blank stare. Enraged, the requester argued with and even struck a fellow builder who was impeding progress. Eventually, a small civil war erupted on the construction site. The men dispersed, the construction project halted permanently and seventy distinct nations and languages ultimately emerged.

It is puzzling: how does such a seemingly small problem as lack of communication stop a lofty project of such tremendous scope?

The French and British jointly finish the Chunnel, the tunnel that connects their two countries, under the English Channel. The variance of language did not stop that great project. Why did a language barrier halt the building of the Tower of Babel?

I once asked my rebbe, Rabbi Mendel Kaplan, of blessed memory, who had escaped from the Nazi inferno to Shanghai, China, where he had lived for nearly five years, how he was able to communicate with the Chinese. He held up a dollar. "Everybody understands this language," he said.

Don't people of different languages manage to communicate when they want to accomplish a noteworthy mission? Why was there no way to marshal the forces, create new communication techniques, and continue the project?

A college professor who was known to give difficult tests had a very lenient policy. If a student missed the exam he could take a make-up test the next day. The make-up, however, was always the same test the professor had given the day before.

Fifteen minutes before the final exam of a particularly difficult course, the professor received a phone call. The four voices crowding the phone booth sounded desperate.

"Professor, we were on our way to take your final and got a flat tire. Please let us take a make-up exam tomorrow."

"Certainly," the professor responded.

The next day the four young men walked in feeling quite smug. They had reviewed the entire final with a friend who had taken it the day before. The professor seated the four students in different corners of the room. Then he placed a single sheet of paper in front of them and stated crisply.

"Today's make-up exam entails just one question. I would like you young men, each in his own words to write down for me" — he looked at the young men and smiled knowingly — "which tire was flat?"

When the goal of a project entails truth and benefits mankind, when the goals are harmonious with concepts that transcend culture, language, custom, or vogue, then nothing can impede success.

But when selfishness rules, and individual glory and gratification are the motivation, then the simplest problem can cause complete disunity, contempt, and, ultimately failure.

When our common goals are based on the common good, then we can unite under the most difficult of circumstances. However, if our motivations are selfish, the slightest impediment will leave our entire mission flat. As flat as the tire of Babel.

PARSHAS
LECH LECHA

🗡 *Mission Impassable*

*T*he news came from a most unlikely source. Og, a feared giant, came to Avraham and informed him that his orphaned nephew Lot was captured in a war. Avraham felt compelled to do something. Lot's father, Haran, was Avraham's younger brother. After Avraham was miraculously saved from death by incineration, Haran, trying to emulate Avraham's monotheistic beliefs, was thrown into a burning furnace.

But miracles don't happen for everyone; and Haran was burned alive.

Now Avraham, the man of peace, was thrust into war. He joined five kings, including the King of S'dom, and battled four of the most powerful kingdoms on Earth. Yet he emerged victorious. He propelled the five kings to a victory that was unprecedented in history. Lot was returned to his family unharmed.

The kings were grateful and they offered Avraham the spoils of war that were rightfully his. Avraham declined their magnanimity. "I lift my hand to Hashem if [I take] so much as a thread to a shoe strap," Avraham replied as he refused to take any personal compensation from the spoils (*Genesis* 14:22).

The question is: if Avraham, when tormented by Pharaoh in Egypt or Avimelech in Grar, had taken gifts as compensation for his humiliation, why did he defer now? What was different about this war that dissuaded Avraham from desiring any rightful financial gain?

Master storyteller, Rabbi Paysach Krohn, tells a beautiful true tale.

One *Shabbos* (Sabbath) afternoon when young Yitzchak Eisenbach was in Jerusalem, he spotted a very valuable gold coin shining in the distance. The value of the coin was enough to support his entire family for two weeks! But it was *Shabbos* and young Yitzele knew that the coin was *muktzeh*, prohibited to be picked up that day. He decided to put his foot on top of the coin and guard it until sunset — a good number of hours, but worth every minute of the wait.

An Arab boy saw Yitzchak with his foot strangely and obviously strategically placed, and decided to investigate further.

"What's that you're hiding?" the boy asked

"Nothing," replied Yitzchak as he shifted his body to hide the fact that he was guarding a golden treasure.

It was too late. The boy pushed him hard, saw the prize, quickly grabbed it and ran away. All Yitzchak could do was watch in horror as the young thief melted into the market place.

Dejected, Yitzchak entered the nearby Tzcernobel *Bais Medrash* (synagogue), where he slumped down in a corner. Normally, Yitzchak helped prepare *Seudah Shlishis*, the final *Shabbos* meal, but that day he sat — dejected and depressed — until *Shabbos* was over. When the Tzcernobel Rebbe inquired about young Yitzchak's sullen mood he was told the story by a few men who had seen the incident.

Immediately after *Shabbos* the Tzcernobel Rebbe summoned Yitzchak into his private study. In his hand he held a gold coin that was exactly the same as the one Yitzchak had almost secured earlier that day.

"I am very proud of you," the Rebbe said. "You did not desecrate the Shabbos even for a tremendous monetary gain. In fact," he continued, "I am so proud of you that I am willing to give you this same coin." The Rebbe paused. "There is one condition. I want you to give me the reward for the mitzvah you did."

The boy looked at the Rebbe in utter disbelief. "You want to trade the coin for the mitzvah?"

The Rebbe nodded slowly.

"If that's the case, keep the coin. I'll keep the mitzvah."

The Rebbe leaned over and kissed the child.

～☆～

Avraham underwent great sacrifice to fight a battle which essentially had nothing to do with him. But he did it for one reason — the *mitzvah* of redeeming his own blood. Avraham refused any compensation that would place a monetary value on the *mitzvah*. Any reward, albeit a strap or thread, would attach a mundane value to an inestimable act.

Pharaoh and Avimelech compensated Avraham for damages — for that he was willing to accept gifts. However, for a priceless *mitzvah* — never! Certain actions we do are beyond physical evaluation. When we keep them in the spheres of the unearthly, they remain like the heavens themselves — eternal.

PARSHAS VAYEIRA

⤳ Masked Bandit

*T*he most exciting news in nearly a century had just come from a most unexpected source. Three angels who had been visiting the home of Avraham and Sora in the guise of Arab nomads, had just spoken a wonderful prophecy: Sora and Avraham were going to have a baby — in one year..

"And Sora laughed at herself, saying, 'After I have withered shall I again rejuvenate? And my husband is old!' (*Genesis* 18.12).

Hashem became upset and asked Avraham, "Why did Sora laugh and claim that she is old? After all, is something beyond My capacities?" (*Genesis* 18:13-14).

What concerns many of the classic commentators is Hashem's obvious deviation from Sora's own words. Sora had blamed the problem on both her own physical state as well aas her husband's advanced age. Yet when Hashem quoted her to Avraham, He substituted Sora's words, "my husband is old" with the words "and I am old," shifting the blame of the situation from Avraham to Sora. Hashem, whose entire essence is that of *emes* (truth), seems to have masked the truth.

❧

When I was two years old, I visited my grandfather, Rabbi Yaakov Kamenetzky, of blessed memory, together with my parents. After a few years as a widower, my grandfather had recently remarried and my step-grandmother was getting used to the new family. I entered the apartment and immediately began playing with items that were not meant to be touched. To distract me, my new grandmother called to me. "What is your name?" she asked.

Beaming like a politician with a prepared response, I shouted, "Bahn-deet Muttel!" Muttel, of course, was a nickname for Mordechai, an affectionate sobriquet that I was called in memory of my mother's grandfather, Reb Boruch Mordechai (Muttel) Burstein.

But *bahn-deet,* a term that in all vernaculars, from Yiddish to English, means bandit, shocked all of the adults. Obviously, someone had labeled me a troublemaker right from the onset of my career.

My mother's face turned beet-red, as her new mother-in-law began chiding her for using derogatory nicknames for children, even in jest.

Before my mother had a chance to defend herself, my grandfather, whose actions through the years had earned him a reputation as a great peacemaker and conciliator par excellence, stepped out of his study. He held his hands out, his palms waving as if to quell the small storm that was brewing. "It's all my fault," he declared.

Everyone looked shocked. In what possible way was the great sage Rabbi Yaakov Kamenetzky, responsible for a two-year-old child running around and declaring himself a bandit?

"Let me explain," my grandfather began. "Young Mordechai is named for his grandfather Boruch Mordechai. However, I asked my son to follow my tradition and give my grandson only one name, as was the custom in Biblical times. That's my opinion, but it is something my daughter-in-law is not accustomed to. To that end, the name Boruch was totally left out.

"I'm sure you are familiar with the name Benedict, or even Bendet," the great sage continued. "Those were Jewish names that were translations of Boruch, just as Wolf is a Yiddish translation of the name Zev and Ber for the Hebrew name Dov. While our daughter-in-law was refused the opportunity to name her son Boruch Mordechai, can we stop her from evoking the affectionate memories she elicits by calling him Bendet Muttel?"

The Talmud tells us that Hashem set a standard for the generations to come. In order to promote peace and harmony within a household, between husbands and wives, one may even stretch the truth. Hashem did not want to quote Sora as saying, "my husband is old." Avraham may have been insulted — even slightly. So Hashem transposed the words as if Sora were talking about herself.

For the sake of peace, if someone errs by insulting another soul, it is no *mitzvah* to quote the affront verbatim — or even accurately. Like Hashem Himself, if one must quote the incident, then he is permitted, even obligated, to hide the truth if it may cause harm to the soul of a Jewish home.

For the sake of *shalom*, it may even be necessary to *mask the bandit*.

PARSHAS
CHAYAI SORA

➣ The Rising Waters of Mentchlichkeit

*A*vraham sent his servant Eliezer on quite a difficult mission: find a suitable *shidach* (match) for not only the world's most eligible bachelor, but also for its most spiritual. Yitzchak, designated by Hashem to be offered as a sacrifice, was also promised to be the progenitor of the nation that would inherit the land that would one day become Israel. In addition, he was raised by the leaders of a generation: the founders of Judaism, Avraham and Sora.

It was not easy to find a match for such a special individual. Avraham made Eliezer promise that he would not bring back a Cannanite woman for his son. Instead, Eliezer was to search among Avraham's family in Charan and find a suitable maiden for the sacrosanct young man.

Laden with gifts, Eliezer left for Charan. As a selection criterion, he devised a sure-fire approach. "Avraham," he thought, "is the epitome of kindness and hospitality. Surely, Avraham would want those qualities prevalent in his daughter-in-law." He prayed to Hashem to guide him. "When I arrive in Charan, I will ask a maiden for water. The maiden who replies by saying, 'Drink, and I shall even give your camels to drink,' must be the one who is designated for Yitzchak" (*Genesis* 24:12-14).

That scenario actually occurred. As Eliezer stood by the well in Charan, Rivka walked toward it. The Torah tells us that as soon as Eliezer watched Rivka begin to draw water, he raced toward her and asked her the pre-determined requests: "Let me sip if you please, a little water from your jug."

Rivka responded graciously by giving him water to drink

and then offering to draw water for all the camels (*Genesis* 24:17-18).

Her gracious response led to our destiny.

The Midrash questions why Eliezer raced forward to greet Rivka. It answers that Eliezer saw a miraculous event as Rivka went to draw water. Before she lowered her bucket, the waters in the well rose to greet her. Therefore, Eliezer ran to greet this maiden, realizing that she was a spiritual individual who must truly be Yitzchak's *bashert* (pre-ordained).

However, if such a miraculous event occurred, why did Eliezer continue with his pre-planned act? Why did he ask Rivka for water and wait until she responded by offering drinks to both him and his entourage? Also, when Eliezer discussed the entire scenario with Rivka's family and told them why he decided upon Rivka, he repeated the story of Rivka's grace and hospitality. Yet Eliezer failed to mention the miraculous incident of the rising waters.

***

In the Slobodka Yeshiva, the study of Torah was of supreme importance, and students who excelled in diligence and ability were viewed with awe. But the greatest reverence was saved for the founder of the yeshiva, Rabbi Nosson Zvi Finkel, the *Alter* of Slobodka. With his brilliance, humility, and remarkable character, he set the tone for the entire yeshiva.

One day, two students were discussing a new young man, Isaac Sher, who had just entered the Yeshiva.

"Isaac is a true *illui* (prodigy)," one said. "He knows the entire *Shas* (Talmud) and *Shulchan Aruch* (Code of Jewish Law) by heart."

After the other boy listened as the first extolled the intellectual virtues of Isaac Sher, he then added meekly, "I had a conversation with him the other day. He is truly a *geshmakeh mentch* (man of character and charm)."

"*Geshmakeh mentch?*" the first student questioned in a scoffing tone. "Is that all you can say about him? We are talking about one of the greatest minds ever to step foot in this Yeshiva, and all you can say is that he is a decent and kind fellow? I see you don't appreciate a person's true value."

With that, the disgusted student sneered and began to walk away, but the towering presence of the *Alter* of Slobodka blocked his path.

"No," he said firmly, motioning to the humiliated student. "That young man is correct. Reb Isaac's greatest quality is that he is a *geshmakeh mentch*."

The *Alter* eventually took Reb Isaac Sher as his son-in-law.

~※~

Eliezer was emotionally impressed by the miraculous rising waters; however, he composed himself. Miracles were not the necessary criteria needed to become Yitzchak's wife. He knew that character transcends any miracle or genius.

In finding the wife of a patriarch and mother of a nation, he did not look for Rivka the miracle worker. He looked, and found, the *geshmakeh mentch*.

PARSHAS TOLDOS

✍ *Butter Battles*

*I*n this *parsha* the Torah tells us of the great dichotomy of character between Yaakov and his older brother Esav. Yaakov sat and studied while Esav hunted. Though it is difficult to understand the roots of this great divide, their parents' reaction to this diversity is even more confusing. The Torah tells us that "Yitzchak loved Esav, for there was game in his mouth; but Rivka loved Yaakov" (*Genesis* 25:28).

The variance in their opinions manifested itself in the fight over the blessings. Yitzchak intended that Esav receive his blessings for worldly goods, intending to save the spiritual blessings for Yaakov. Yet Rivka pushed Yaakov to attain the blessings for the worldly goods, too.

What was the fundamental difference between Yitzchak's and Rivka's views of their children? Why was there such a diverse notion as to which son should inherit the wealth of this world? How is it possible that Yitzchak, who epitomized the very essence of spirituality, favored Esav, a man steeped in worldly desires?

✍

Vice President Al Gore tells a story about New Jersey Senator Bill Bradley. Senator Bradley once attended a dinner at which he was a guest speaker. The waiter set down a side dish of potatoes and placed a pat of butter upon them. The Senator asked for an extra portion of butter. "I'm sorry, sir," the very unyielding server replied tersely, "one pat per guest."

With a combined expression of shock, scorn, and disbelief, Senator Bradley looked up at the formal steward. "Excuse me," he said. "Do you know who I am? I am New Jersey Senator Bill Bradley." The Senator cleared his throat. "I am a Rhodes scholar and a former NBA star. I currently serve on the International Trade and Long-Term Growth Committee, and the Debt and Deficit Reduction Committee, and I am in charge of Taxation and IRS Oversight. And I'd like another pat of butter on my potatoes."

The waiter looked down at the Senator. "Do you know who I am?" he asked. "I am the one in charge of the butter."

Yitzchok understood the great contrariety between his children. However, he felt that Esav, the hunter-child, understood the mundane world far better. So it was only fitting that Esav be gifted with the blessings of this world. Esav would then supplement Yaakov's needs, and a true symbiosis would emerge. Rivka, on the other hand, was pragmatic: she felt that putting Esav in charge of the material world would lead to Esav's selfish hoarding, and consequently Yaakov would barely receive a portion.

Rivka understood that while Yaakov's sustenance was basically spiritual, he still needed a little butter to survive. She knew that she could not rely on Esav controlling the butter: she knew his personality all too well. There would be no parity or sharing; Esav would take it all.

Everybody has a job, whether it be spiritual or menial, and each job must be executed with a sense of responsibility and mission. The argument between Rivka and Yitzchak was complex, but it was simple, too. Esav may have been more astute in churning the butter; however, would he make sure to give Yaakov his fair share? Rivka knew that the world would be a better place if her two sons shared their respective portions. But she wouldn't count on it. For unless Esav knew how to give an appropriate pat, a fair and suitable share, he could not be in charge of the butter.

PARSHAS VAYEITZEI

✒ A Train to Nowhere

t just doesn't make sense. After more than twenty years of toiling in the house of Lavan, Yaakov wanted out. He certainly was entitled. After all, he had married Lavan's daughters in exchange for years of tending the sheep, and he had increased Lavan's livestock population manyfold. Additionally, he had been a faithful son-in-law despite his conniving huckster father-in-law. Yet when Yaakov left Lavan's home with his wives, children, and flocks, he snuck out, fearing that Lavan would never let him leave. Then Yaakov was pursued by Lavan, who chased him with a vengeance. But Yaakov was blessed, for Hashem appeared to Lavan in a dream and warned him not to harm Yaakov. Eventually, Lavan overtook Yaakov and accosted him. "Why have you led my daughters away like captives of the sword? Why have you fled, secretly, without notifying me? Had you told me you wanted to leave I would have sent you off with song and music!" (*Genesis* 31:26-27).

Yaakov answered his father-in-law by declaring his fear: "You would have stolen your daughters from me." Lavan then searched all of Yaakov's belongings, looking for idols missing from his collection. Yaakov was outraged; he simply did not understand what Lavan wanted. Yaakov responded to the abuse by detailing the enormous amount of selfless work (through scorching heat and freezing nights) that he slaved to make Lavan a wealthy man. Reviewing the care and concern that he always had for his wives and children, Yaakov declared that he was not worthy of the mean-spirited attacks made by his father-in-law. "And," Yaakov told Lavan, "if not for the protection of Hashem, you would have sent me away empty-handed" (*Genesis* 31:38-42).

Yet Lavan was unmoved. Like a stoic, unyielding dictator, Lavan responded, "The daughters are my daughters, the children are my children, the flock is my flock, and all that you see is mine" (*Genesis* 31:43).

What could have gone on in Lavan's mind? What motivates a man to be so selfish and unreasonable?

Rabbi Dr. Abraham Twerski of Pittsburgh tells the story of the small European *shtetl* that heard about a marvelous new invention — the locomotive. The government was offering to put a station in the town, but taxes would have to be raised. Skeptical about the concept of a horseless carriage, the townsfolk sent an emissary to a nearby village that had just completed a set of tracks on which the new-fangled modern miracle was set to travel. Getzel, the emissary, had one mission: to verify the existence of such a machine and explain its mechanics to the entire town. They would then vote whether or not to accept the train in their midst.

Getzel returned home in awe. He had learned the principles of the machine and was determined to convince the townsfolk to accept the offer. Equipped with diagrams and working models of the train, he explained the concepts of a steam engine. For hours he explicated and demonstrated the workings of the engine, pistons, and levers. Finally, almost everyone agreed — the train was a true marvel and would be a great benefit to the town.

But one man had other ideas. He jumped from his seat. "Bah! Feh! It's all a trick!" the man exclaimed. "How can something run without a horse? It just can't be!"

Getzel was prepared. He began the entire presentation over again. He even showed the skeptic a working model of a train. Then he boiled water and fascinated the crowd by showing how the model train actually moved. Even the doubter was shaking his head in amazement.

"It's truly amazing," he nodded in submission. "It really does work. But tell me, just where do you attach the horses?"

<hr>

Lavan just wouldn't get it. No matter how clearly Yaakov explained his case, twenty years of work, devoted labor under the worst conditions, Lavan was unmoved. "The daughters are my daughters, the children are my children, and whatever you have is mine," he said.

When the sickness of self-indulgence overtakes the emotional stability of a human soul, you can talk, you can cajole, and you can persuade. The Almighty can even appear to you in a dream and do His part. But it is hopeless. Unless a person actually takes the initiative to realize his shortcomings, anything that anyone may tell him is only a train to nowhere.

PARSHAS VAYISHLACH

➤ Clueless in Canaan

One of the Torah's most famous battles was not between two armies or two nations. It was between mortal man and his immortal counterpart — an angel.

As he left his family's encampment to retrieve some small items, Yaakov lingered alone in the pre-dawn hours, and a man approached him. The man engaged him in battle, and in the struggle, Yaakov dislocated his hip socket. Nevertheless, he was able to lock the mysterious man in a fast hold. "Send me away," the foe cried, "dawn is approaching."

Yaakov realized that this combatant was no ordinary wayfarer; in fact, he was a heavenly messenger — the Angel of Esav — and Yaakov made a condition for release. "I will not release you unless you bless me," he demanded (*Genesis* 32:27).

The Midrash explains that everyone has an angelic representative. Yaakov, who had Divine inspiration, met his angelic opponent as a prelude to the face-to-face encounter with his adversarial mortal brother. The Talmud explains that the angel had celestial responsibilities that began at dawn. He therefore begged Yaakov to allow him to return to those duties.

In response to Yaakov's demand, the angel asked Yaakov his name, to which the angel declared, "Your name will no longer be Yaakov but rather Yisrael (Israel), as you fought with angels and with men (Lavan & Esav) — and won" (*Genesis* 32:28-29).

Then Yaakov asked the angel for his name. The response was enigmatic. "Why do you ask my name?" There was no further response. The angel blessed Yaakov who, badly injured, limped back to his family (*Genesis* 32:30-32).

The obvious question is: What is the meaning of the angel's response? Why did he answer Yaakov's question with a question? Why did he refuse to divulge his name? Or did the angel actually give an answer to Yaakov with that question?

～～✦～～

At our supper table one evening each of our children took turns trying to stump me and my wife, with riddles. Some of the brain twisters were quite tricky, but my wife and I managed to figure out the answers. Then my daughter announced that she had something to say that would stump everyone.

After prefacing her remarks by telling everyone to listen to the clues carefully, she started her riddle.

She began by telling us that China had 1.2 billion people, it occupied approximately 3,700,000 square miles, and its population density was 327 people per square mile. She continued by listing China's principal languages: Mandarin, Yue, Wu, Hakka, Xiang, Gan, Minbei, and Minnan.

Then she stopped, and with a probing tone in her voice declared quite quizzically: "How long is a Chinese person's name."

We all took the last statement as a question and looked at each other. We were stumped. How did the previously stated facts correlate with the length of a Chinese person's name? How would the fact that China had over a billion people explain how long a Chinese name was?

Again she stood up and repeated: "How long is a Chinese person's name."

In unison, we all shrugged our shoulders. "O.K.," we conceded, "How long is a Chinese person's name?"

My daughter just smiled. "I don't know either. I never asked you a question. All I wanted to tell you, in addition to all the other facts that I mentioned about China, is that How Long is the name of a Chinese person!"

Sometimes, "why do you ask" is a question; sometimes it is an answer as well. The angel that wrestled with Yaakov responded to Yaakov's question in a very intriguing way. My name is "why do you ask my name." Rabbi Yehuda Laib Chasman, of blessed memory, the *Mashgiach* (dean of ethics) of the Chevron Yeshiva, explained that the angel of Esau delivered a very poignant message. Esav's motto is, "Why do you ask?" If we do not ask questions, Esav's angel will surely overcome. If you ask no questions, no answers are necessary. Actions go unchecked, and there is never an accounting.

Throughout history, Jews always asked for names. When Moshe first encountered God in the wilderness he asked of Him, "When the Jews ask me what is His Name what should I tell them?" Hashem responds, "I Shall Be As I Shall Be" (*Exodus* 3:13-14). The Jews were asking for an anthropomorphic quality that God's name personified. Yaakov, too, wanted to understand the very essence of the angel who personified the struggles he would eternally encounter.

The answer was simple — My name is "Why-do-you-ask-my-name." That name may be a little confusing at times. It may be difficult to comprehend. It may even sound Chinese. But if we don't ask, and if we are satisfied with the response, "why do you even ask?", then we will never have an answer. In fact, we won't even have a clue.

PARSHAS VAYEISHEV

✒ *Forget Me — Not!!*

ear the end of this *parsha*, the Torah tells how Yoseph was falsely accused of adultery and was sent to prison. During Yoseph's detention the Torah tells us "Hashem was with Yoseph. He was endowed with charm and had much favor in the eyes of the warden. In fact, the warden placed all the other prisoners in Yoseph's custody, and Yoseph was in charge of all their duties. The warden trusted everything that Yoseph did, and because Hashem was with him everything that he (Yoseph) discharged was successful" (*Genesis* 39:21-23).

In addition to the Divine Providence that cloaked Yoseph, another striking incident occurred. Back at the palace, Pharaoh was served wine with an insect floating in it, and a foreign substance was baked into his bread. The baker and butler were both jailed for these breaches and were placed in Yoseph's charge. After a year in prison, they both dreamt a strange dream. Yoseph, Divinely guided, interpreted each dream with amazing accuracy. He predicted that the baker would be executed for his infraction, while the butler would be returned to his former position.

Yoseph, convinced of the power of his predictions, did not stop with mere interpretations. He then implored the butler to discuss his own plight with Pharaoh. "If only you would think of me when Pharaoh benefits you, and mention me to Pharaoh, then you will get me out of here," Yoseph pleaded (*Genesis* 40:14). Yet Yoseph erred. The butler completely ignored Yoseph's requests and left him to languish in prison for another two years. In fact, upon mentioning Yoseph to Pharaoh, the butler even referred to him in a very disparaging manner.

The Midrash explains that the butler's response, or lack thereof, was a heavenly punishment. Yoseph should not have placed his trust in a mortal man and urged him to be the conduit for his release. Instead, he should have placed his faith in Hashem. Many commentaries question this Midrash, asking, "is it not one's duty to employ the help of others? Why should Yoseph have relied solely on Hashem? What is wrong with asking for help from below instead of relying solely on the One Above?"

My grandfather, Rabbi Yaakov Kamenetzky, of blessed memory, had a keen sense of direction, not only in spiritual life, but in mundane matters like city streets as well. He was once in a car with a colleague, a *Rosh Yeshiva* (dean) of a prestigious Yeshiva. That particular *Rosh Yeshiva* happened to be a nervous individual and unfortunately panicked when the driver, a student of his, lost his way in an area of the city that did not generally welcome rabbis with open arms. Understandably, the young man wanted desperately to get back on the highway.

"Please," pleaded the Rosh Yeshiva of his student, "*freg a politzmahn* (ask a policeman)!"

Reb Yaakov interrupted. "You needn't ask. I know the way." Reb Yaakov turned his attention to the driver. "Continue for two blocks, make a left. After the first light, you make another left. Make an immediate right, and you will see the entrance to the highway."

Reb Yaakov's colleague was not convinced. "Please," he insisted of the driver, "ask a policeman!"

The student felt obliged to listen to his *Rosh Yeshiva* and spotted a police car on the other side of the street, two blocks away. Quickly, he made a U-turn, drove the two blocks, and stopped the officer. "Excuse me, officer," asked the nervous driver, "how do you get back on the Brooklyn-Queens Expressway?"

The officer saw the two sages in the back seat of the car and realized the urgency of the situation. He proceeded to give directions. "First of all, turn back around and go four blocks. Then make a left. After the first light, you make another left. Make an immediate right and you will see the entrance to the Brooklyn-Queens Expressway."

My grandfather turned to his colleague and smiled. "Nu, my friend," whispered Reb Yaakov, "now that the gentile said it, do you feel better?"

~*~

Rabbi Moshe Feinstein, of blessed memory (who incidentally was not the other *Rosh Yeshiva*), explains that there are two types of individuals. There are those who have no heavenly signs, and so the thought of Hashem is quite remote from them. Then there are those whose every action is blessed with the guidance of a spiritual force. It is almost as if Hashem is walking hand in hand with them, or even as if Hashem is sitting next to them. Yoseph should have realized that the events that transpired in the prison cell were Divine. Within one year of entering prison, he was charged with the welfare of every prisoner. Then two Egyptian stewards were sent to be with him, and each had a dream that the Divinely inspired Yoseph interpreted in prophetic fashion. At that point, Yoseph should have understood that his freedom was imminent. Hashem, through His own mysterious yet miraculous ways, would surely get him out of jail. The butler was extremely impressed when Yoseph's interpretation proved correct. But Yoseph did not have to implore him twice with requests for mercy. When Hashem is the navigator, there is no need to ask for directions.

PARSHAS MIKEITZ

~ Dreamers & Doers

*I*n this portion Yoseph was transformed from a brutalized, libeled, and mocked slave into the Viceroy of Egypt, the world's most powerful nation. In a matter of moments Yoseph, derided as a Hebrew slave, was elevated by Pharaoh to second-in-command and held the key to the world's food supply.

Let us analyze the events that led to this rise in power. Pharaoh dreamt a bizarre scene. Seven fat cows were devoured by seven lean ones. Seven diseased wheat stalks consumed seven healthy ones. There was no trace of either the fat cows or robust stalks. Pharaoh woke up very disturbed. What could it mean?

Not one of Pharaoh's advisers was able to interpret the dreams in a meaningful manner. Pharaoh's butler recalled his own strange dream of two years back. He told Pharaoh that a Hebrew slave interpreted it accurately. Perhaps it would be worthwhile to consult him.

Pharaoh released Yoseph from jail and narrated the dream to him. Yoseph, after stating that it is Hashem who interprets all dreams, explained that seven years of famine would ultimately come and devour seven years of plenty that would precede them. The famine was to be so powerful that the years of plenty would vanish without a trace. Like the fat cows and healthy stalks that were devoured without a sign, there would be no trace of the good times.

What happened next is startling. As if on cue, Yoseph began to counsel Pharaoh, the ruler of the most powerful nation on earth, exactly how to preempt the imminent disaster. "And now Pharaoh shall appoint a wise and discerning man who will oversee the seven years of plenty." Yoseph then devised a plan to store the bounty of the good years in order to preserve it for the famine. He also arranged a method of distribution to the population (*Genesis* 41:33-37). Yoseph was extremely blessed. Pharaoh picked him as the "wise and discerning man!"

Upon reading this section, I was amazed. Yoseph's interpretations followed rejections of a host of other interpretations, all presented by advisers who were well acquainted with the king. Yet Yoseph, a lowly newcomer, who had received his first bath and haircut only moments earlier, supplemented his interpretation by declaring to the King of Egypt exactly how to resolve the ensuing problems. This happened even before the king acknowledged his approval of the dream's interpretations! How dare this slave, released hours ago from prison, offer his advice on domestic agricultural policy to the foremost ruler of the world?

~~~

A young American who was engaged to an Israeli girl entered the study of the Gerrer Rebbe in Jerusalem. "I am soon to be married and have no friends or relatives in Israel. I was told that the Rebbe has insight in these matters. Perhaps the Rebbe can guide me in my decision." The young man laid some architectural plans on the table, and the Rebbe peered at them intently. After a few moments, the Rebbe suggested a few changes that the soon-to-be-married fellow understood. However, he was not sure if he would be able to convey these changes to the Israeli builder.

The young man returned elated to his Yeshiva that afternoon. A few of his friends were astonished, not only that he gathered up the courage to discuss a mundane apartment with a great *tzaddik*, but that the Rebbe gave him time and advice in the matter. The young man searched the Yeshiva for someone who was fluent in *Ivrit* to accompany him to discuss the changes with the architect. A few days later, he went to the building site accompanied by an Israeli friend who began to explain the Rebbe's suggestions to him.

The builder's face turned white. "How do you know about these suggestions? The Rebbe of Ger was

here just a few days ago and made the same suggestions. He said it would improve every house in the
development. How do you know about these suggestions?"

—✦—

Yoseph understood the challenge that lay before him. It
would be thoughtless and irresponsible only to interpret the
dream and then walk away. If he had the solution to the problem, it was his duty to suggest it. This approach was not without
risk. Pharaoh might have considered him a *yenta*. How dare a
lowly slave with intuitive powers tell the King of Egypt how to
conduct domestic policy! However, Yoseph went beyond his ini-
tial calling. He felt that if the whole solution to the problem were
in his hands, then withholding it was just as rash as misinter-
preting the dream.

When the ball is thrown your way you must do more than
just catch it. You have to carry it.

PARSHAS VAYIGASH

✒ Destiny Today

*T*he plot thickens. At the end of the last *parsha*, Yoseph had accused his brothers of stealing his special silver goblet. Yehuda, in charge of the troupe, had denied even the remotest possibility that any one of the brothers could be a thief. Yehuda was so confident that he had pre-judged any so-called thief to a death penalty and had offered the remaining group of nine brothers as slaves should the egregious accusations prove correct. Unfortunately, Yehuda had been unaware of Yoseph's pre-contrived ruse of planting the goblet in Binyamin's sack. This portion begins with Yehuda stepping forward to intercede on Binyamin's behalf after Yoseph insisted that Binyamin, and only Binyamin, remain as a slave. This turn of events was something that Yehuda would battle and risk his life to prevent.

As Yoseph and Yehuda confronted each other, Yehuda appealed with a mixed array of rage, fury, and emotions. Bargaining with Yoseph, nearly threatening war over the matter, Yehuda explained that Binyamin could not be taken as a slave, as he had left an old father who awaited his return. If he would not return to his father, the old man would die of grief and aggravation. After all, he already lost one son to a terrible accident (*Genesis* 44:22-34).

After seeing the concern that Yehuda had for his younger brother, Yoseph made a startling revelation. "I am Joseph. Is my father still alive?" (*Genesis* 45:3). Yoseph then forgave the brothers and told them that his unfortunate displacement was divinely preordained to arrange their lifeline during the ensuing famine. Before Yoseph sent his brothers back to Canaan to bring their father to Egypt, he presented each of his brothers with a set of clothes. But when it came to his youngest brother Binyamin, Yoseph did more. He gave Binyamin five sets of clothing and three hundred pieces of silver (*Genesis* 45:22). The Talmud (*Megilah* 16b) asks a very poignant question. How is it that Yoseph, a victim of jealousy, now provoked his brothers by favoring Binyamin? Didn't favoritism spur the hatred that led to the original calamity? Why didn't Yoseph learn from his own past experience not to show favoritism?

The Talmud explains that Yoseph was very calculating in his actions. In fact, Yoseph was alluding to a similar event that would occur in the future. After being saved from the gallows, Mordechai, a descendant of Binyamin, miraculously rose to power and prestige. He, too, was given a gift of a wardrobe of five sets of clothing as he left the palace of Achashveirosh. So Binyamin's five changes of clothing were symbolic of a future sartorial gift that his descendant would one day receive.

Some commentaries ask powerful questions. Obviously, Yoseph did not explain the deep meaning of his actions to his brothers. What then was gained by favoring Binyamin in front of them? Would the symbolic reference — which might not be clear to them all — negate any ill feeling? Would some mysterious token resolve a problem that may have been simmering? Why did Yoseph, in the midst of the turmoil of his startling revelation, decide to make a ceremonial gift that favored one brother over the others in order to foreshadow an event destined to occur more than 1,000 years in the future? Could he not have saved symbolism for a more copacetic setting?

—✦—

Rabbi Paysach Krohn tells a beautiful tale in his book *Along the Maggid's Journey*. In 1939, the Gestapo shut down Rabbi Moshe Schneider's yeshiva in Frankfurt, Germany. With great effort and generous support from the English Jewish community, he was able to relocate the school to England.

Survival during that horrific period was both an enormous spiritual and physical challenge, but two boys in the yeshiva helped. They both were named Moshe. One Moshe would rise in the early hours of the morning and pick up leftover bread from a generous bakery. Carrying the bags of bread and leftover rolls while walking through the bitter cold was not easy, but Moshe never missed his duties. In fact, he often took the place of other boys who were supposed to do this chore.

The other Moshe also woke up early. He led a special learning session before dawn, encouraging his friends to make the extra effort — which they religiously did.

After years of uninterrupted service, one day the boys received public recognition. Rabbi Schneider blessed them in front of the entire school. "Moshe who *schleps* the bread is not only *schlepping* today's bread. One day, he will help distribute bread for thousands of people. And the Moshe who is concerned with the spirituality of others will continue to do so in the years to come. Their actions today are only the seeds of the future."

His words proved true. Moshe, the bread-*schlepper*, became Moshe (Paul) Reichman, one of our generation's most benevolent philanthropists. Moshe, the young teacher, became Rabbi Moshe Sternbuch, Rav in Johannesburg, South Africa and Har Nof, Israel, a noted halachic authority, author of prestigious books on Jewish law, and teacher of thousands.

～✦～

Perhaps Yoseph was telling us the secret of our people. Binyamin stood in shackles. Accused of stealing a goblet, he was humiliatingly sentenced to life-long enslavement to Pharaoh. Moments later, he was liberated and recognized with honor as the blood brother, who shared both mother and father, of the most powerful man in the world. Yoseph gave the former slave-to-be a special five-fold gift as an announcement to the world. Through Binyamin, Yoseph declared the future of our people — that today's events are our manifest destiny. Due to the courageous actions of Yehuda, Binyamin, the slave-to-be, walked away triumphantly, not with one change of clothing but with five. This was not a symbol for some event that would occur a thousand years in the future, but rather a symbol of the ever-present character of the Jewish people.

As such, the episode of Binyamin in Egypt manifested itself in direct comparison and beautiful symmetry with events that occurred centuries later in Persia. Mordechai the *Yehudi*, a descendant of Binyamin, stood his ground before threats of death and humiliation. He defied the prophets of doom and walked away with glory and splendor. Yoseph's message was no riddle, it was no illusion, and it was no mystical prophecy: It was our destiny. Courage in trying times yields greatness. This was not a message only *for* the future. It was a message *of* the future, for today, that all the brothers could appreciate — at that moment. It is a message we too can appreciate — right now.

PARSHAS VAYECHI

➤ Stand & Deliver

*T*his week's *parsha* marks the end of the Book of *Braishis* (*Genesis*). Yaakov summoned his son Yoseph and discussed final arrangements with him. He asked to be transported to Chevron and to be interred in the same cave as his father, mother, and grandparents. Yoseph returned home, and an unprecedented event occurred — Yaakov took ill. He is the first human that the Torah records as getting sick. Yoseph was informed and quickly hurried to his father's bedside. The Torah tells us that when Yoseph was announced, "Israel (Jacob) exerted himself and sat up on the bed" (*Genesis* 48:2). Yoseph entered the room and Yaakov proceeded to recount the major events of his life to him. Yaakov talked about his Divine revelations and the blessings that the Almighty bestowed upon him. He discussed the death of Rachel and explained why he buried her in Bais Lechem and not Chevron. Then Yaakov proceeded to bless his beloved son Yoseph's children in a unique manner. He designated Yoseph's children as *shevatim* (tribes) with equal rights and inheritance as his other sons.

One portion of the episode needs clarification. The Torah is usually short on detail. Why then does the Torah tell us that when Yoseph walked in Yaakov exerted himself and sat up in bed? Why is that significant? Who cares if he sat up or lay down? If he was able to sit, why should he not? And if it was very difficult for him to sit up, why did he? And isn't *what* Yaakov said more relevant than *how* he said it?

Rashi explains that this seemingly supplementary detail teaches us a lesson. A father whose son has risen to power must show respect. It may have been quite difficult for Yaakov to sit, however it was important. One must show respect for royalty, even if it is his own child who has risen to power. I'd like to analyze the incident from another angle.

~~~

American historian Paul F. Boller Jr., relates the following story: At noon on January 1, 1863, the final draft of the Emancipation Proclamation was placed in front of Abraham Lincoln. He stared intensely at it as it lay before him on his desk. He picked up his pen to sign it, and was about to dip the quill into the ink when he hesitated and put his arm down. He paused, closed his eyes, and began the process again. Determinedly he picked up the quill, dipped it in the ink, and put it down. With a grim face he turned to Secretary of State William N. Seward and said, "My hands have been shaking since nine o'clock this morning. My right hand is almost paralyzed. If I am ever to go down in history, it will be for this act. My whole self is in it. However, if my hand trembles when I sign this proclamation, whoever examines it will say hereafter, 'he hesitated.'"

With that, the President composed himself, dipped the quill into the ink, and slowly but resolutely signed in perfect form — Abraham Lincoln.

~~~

As he lay on his deathbed, Yaakov was about to perform an unprecedented act. He was about to bestow the title of *shevatim*, tribes, to his grandchildren Ephraim and Menashe. This was an honor only relegated to his own children. Then he blessed them with words that were destined to become the hallmark of paternal blessings for generations to come: "By you shall (the children of) Israel bless their children — May God make you like Ephraim and Menashe" (*Genesis* 48:20).

Such blessings could not be endowed while lying down. As weak as Yaakov was, he knew that the future of two young tribes lay in the strength of his blessing. He wouldn't give it lying down. Our patriarch Yaakov knew that displaying any sign of weakness while transferring that most important message would be recognized for eternity. Therefore, he mustered his strength and sat up to give the blessing that would wax eternal. Execution of great actions needs great strength and fortitude. Our forefather Yaakov knew that just as there are things you can't *take* lying down, there are also many things, namely greatness and blessing, that you cannot *give* lying down.

ספר שמות

The Book of
Exodus

PARSHAS SHEMOS

≫ *Balance of Power*

"*I*f nominated, I shall not accept — if elected, I shall not serve." The words of Civil War General George Tecumseh Sherman ring clear in American history as a tribute to a man's obstinate unwillingness to commit to further service to a shattered country.

It seems that Moshe responded in nearly the same manner, not to a nominating committee but to God Almighty. When Moshe was approached by Hashem to speak to Pharaoh, he deferred. First Moshe pondered, "Who am I to go to Pharaoh?" (*Exodus* 3:11). After Hashem exhorted him, Moshe tried a different tactic. "I am not a man of words . . . I am heavy of mouth and speech." Again, God refuted his excuses, chiding Moshe that, after all, "who makes a mouth for man if not the Almighty?" Once again, He urged Moshe to go to Pharaoh, assuring him that "I will be with your mouth and teach you what to say" (*Exodus* 4:10-12).

When Hashem seemingly convinced Moshe by assuring him that His hand would guide him, His words would be spoken, and His spirit would inspire him, Moshe still did not accept. He had one final pretext: "Send whomever You will send" (*Exodus* 4:13).

The scenario is almost incomprehensible. After every one of Moshe's protestations were well refuted by the Almighty, how did Moshe have the seeming audacity to petition God to send someone else?

≫≪

My second-grade rebbe, Rabbi Chaim Follman, asked his *Rosh Yeshiva*, Rabbi Yaakov Kamenetzky, to

officiate at the wedding of his daughter. Reb Yaakov checked his appointment calendar and shook his head slowly. "Unfortunately I have a prior commitment and cannot fulfill your request." He then wished Reb Chaim and his daughter a heartfelt *mazel tov*, showered them with blessings, and added that if his schedule happened to change, he would gladly join them at the wedding.

On the day of the wedding, Reb Yaakov was informed that his original appointment was canceled. Immediately, he made plans to attend the wedding. Assuming he would come after the ceremony, he arrived at the hall long after the time that the invitation had announced that the ceremony would commence.

Upon entering the wedding hall, Reb Yaakov realized that for one reason or another the *chupah* (marriage ceremony) had not yet begun. Quickly, Reb Yaakov went downstairs and waited, almost in hiding, near the coat room for nearly 40 minutes until after the ceremony was completed. A few students who noticed the *Rosh Yeshiva* huddled in a corner reciting *Tehillim* (Psalms) could not imagine why he was not upstairs and participating in the *chupah*. However, they did not approach him until after the ceremony.

Reb Yaakov explained his actions. "Surely, Reb Chaim had made arrangements for a different *m'sader kidushin* (officiating rabbi). Had he known that I was in the wedding hall, he would be in a terrible bind — after all, I was his first choice, and I am much older than his second choice. Reb Chaim would be put in the terribly uncomfortable position of asking someone to defer his honor to me. Then Reb Chaim would have to placate that rabbi with a different honor, thus displacing someone else. And so on. I therefore felt that the best thing to do was stay in a corner until the entire ceremony had ended — sparing everybody the embarrassment of even the slightest demotion."

Moshe's older brother Ahron had been the prophet of the Jewish nation, guiding them, encouraging them, and supporting them for decades before Moshe was asked by Hashem to go to Pharaoh. When Moshe was finally convinced by the Almighty that he was worthy of the designated mission, and that his speech impediment was not an inhibiting factor, there was one more issue with which Moshe had to deal. This matter would not be resolved with heavenly intervention. It was a very mortal factor — his brother Ahron's feelings. It would be extremely difficult, even if every other qualification were met, for Moshe to accept a position that might, in some way, slight his brother Ahron.

Only after Moshe was assured of Ahron's overwhelming support and willingness to forego his previous status did Moshe accept the great task. Sanctity of mission and divinity of assignment end somewhere very sacred: at the tip of someone else's heart.

PARSHAS VA'EIRA

➤ Hitting Pay Dirt

*T*here is a certain sensitivity displayed in this portion that serves as a lesson to mankind. The first two of the Ten Plagues that befell Egypt involved water. In the first plague, the waters of Egypt turned into blood. The second plague had frogs emerge from the water. In order to generate those miraculous events, Moshe's staff had to strike the waters. Moshe, however, did not do it. He was told that his brother Ahron should do the striking. After all, the waters of the Nile had been Moshe's refuge when as a three-month-old child he was hidden in a reed basket from Pharoah's soldiers who were drowning all Jewish babies. It would therefore not be fitting for one who was saved by the water to strike it.

The next plague, lice, emerged from the earth. After the earth was struck with Moshe's staff, lice emerged, afflicting all of Egypt. Again Moshe was told not to be the active agent. After all, he had to be grateful to the earth that had hidden the Egyptian whom he had killed.

Of course, the great ethicists derive the importance of gratitude from Moshe's behavior. "Imagine," they point out, "Moshe had to refrain from striking inanimate objects because he was saved by them many years prior! How much more must we show gratitude to living beings who have been our vehicles of good fortune!"

Such ideas are correct, of course, but why is striking water or earth a display of ingratitude? Was it not the will of Hashem to have the waters and dust converted? Would it not be a great elevation to those waters or that dust to be transformed to higher components of God's glory? That being the case, wouldn't it be most fitting that Moshe be chosen to elevate such simple waters or lowly dirt into objects that declare the open presence of an Almighty Creator who shouts together with his humble servant, "Let My people serve Me?"

Rabbi Nosson Schapira of Krakow once told of his most difficult case.

A wealthy merchant from Warsaw would do business each month in the Krakow market. On each visit he noticed an extremely pious widow huddled near her basket of bread reciting *Tehillim* (Psalms). She only lifted her eyes from her worn prayer book to sell a roll. After each sale she would then shower her customer with a myriad of blessings and immediately return to the frayed pages which were moistened with teardrops and devotion.

Upon observing her each month, the Krakow businessman came to a conclusion. "This pious woman should not have to struggle to earn a living," he said. "She should be able to pursue her prayers and piety with no worries."

He then offered to double her monthly earnings on one condition: she would leave the bread business and spend her time in the service of the Lord. The woman, tears of joy streaming down her face, accepted the generous offer and thanked the kind man with praise, gratitude, and blessing.

A month later, when the man returned to Krakow, he was shocked to find the woman at her usual place, mixing the sweet smell of rolls with the sweet words of *Tehillim*. As soon as he approached, the woman handed him an envelope. "Here is your money", she said simply. "I thought it over and I can't accept your offer."

"A deal is a deal," he exclaimed. "We must see Rabbi Schapira!"

After the businessman presented his case, the woman spoke. "The reason this generous man offered to support me was to help me grow in spirituality and devotion," she explained. "From the day I left my bread business I've only fallen. Let me explain.

"Every day that it would rain, I would think of the farmers who planted the wheat for my bread and rolls. I would sing praises for the glory of rain, as I felt the personal guidance of Hashem with each raindrop. When the sun would shine, I would once again thank Hashem for permitting the farmers to harvest in good weather. When I ground the flour and then sifted it, I'd find countless reasons to thank the Almighty. When the bread baked golden brown I'd thank Hashem for the beauty of the product and its sweet smell. And when a customer would come I'd thank both Hashem for sending him and then bless my patron, too! Now, this is all gone, and I want no part of a simple, all-expenses-paid life."

Moshe had a very personal relationship with the water and the dust. Each time he saw the Nile or trod upon the ground, he remembered the vehicles of his blessings and used them to praise Hashem. Blood, frogs, and lice are surely miraculous, but they were not Moshe's personal salvation. Striking the water or earth may have produced great national miracles, but Moshe would be left without the simple dirt that yielded great choruses of personal praise. For when one forgoes marveling at a lowly speck of dust and chooses instead to focus upon huge mountains, he may never hit pay dirt. He may only bite the dust.

PARSHAS BO

☞ Out of Africa

*I*magine that you are a tourist on your way to see this nation's most revered document, the one that forged our beliefs and principles. You enter the hallowed halls of the Library of Congress and ask a guard, "Which way to the Declaration of Independence?" He points to a sign with bold letters, a large arrow, and the words "This way to the *Declaratsiya o Nezavisimossti.*" Then, in small print, the sign translates the two Russian words — Declaration of Independence.

You would be shocked. Why in the world would the United States government use a foreign language to identify the very document that symbolizes the essence of America? Of course, this story is not true and could never happen.

So how do we understand the Torah's choice of words to introduce the most Jewish of all symbols — *tefillin.* The Torah commands that the Children of Israel wear *tefillin* and uses a very unique expression: "They shall be for *totafos* between your eyes" (*Exodus* 13:16). The Talmud in *Sanhedrin* is concerned with the etymology of the word *totafos,* for clearly it has no Jewish origin. The Talmud then declares that *totafos* is a compound word made up of two foreign words. The word *tot* in Kotpi means two, and the word *fas* in Afriki (I assume an African dialect) also means two. The *tefillin* on the head is comprised of four compartments: thus, *tot-fas* or *totafos* meaning four.

How baffling! Why would the Torah use a compound of two very foreign words to describe a Jewish — perhaps the most Jewish — symbol?

What is even more interesting is that just a few verses prior, the Torah refers to the *tefillin* boxes as a *zikaron* (*remembrance*) between the eyes (*Exodus* 13:9). If the Torah calls *tefillin* a remembrance, then why does it refer to them as *totafos*? Moreover, if they are *totafos,* then why call them a remembrance?

Stephen Savitsky, CEO of Staff Builders, one of America's leading home health care providers, spends quite a bit of time travelling on airplanes. It is at 35,000 feet that he has met Jews of great diversity, backgrounds, and beliefs. Once, on a flight out of Baton Rouge toward Wichita, Kansas, he was bumped to first class where he found himself seated next to a large man with a thick gold ring on his pinkie and an even thicker gold chain hanging loosely from his neck. The man was chewing an unlit cigar while immersing himself in a sports magazine. As soon as the seat belt sign was turned off he ordered two drinks. While the seemingly flamboyant jet-setter was immersed in his own self, he hardly glanced at the neatly groomed executive sitting next to him. The man surely did not notice that Steve's head was covered during the entire flight.

When the flight attendants began serving the meal, the smell of glazed ham that was wafting from his neighbor's tray made it difficult for Steve to eat his kosher food. It was only after the meals were cleared and the trays removed that Steve took out a small *siddur* (prayer book) to say Grace After Meals.

All of a sudden a pair of eyes were transfixed on the *siddur*. "Hey, my friend!" exclaimed the man, and Steve heard a Brooklyn accent cowering underneath the Southern drawl, "is that a *seedoor*?" Steve nodded, "Sure. Do you want to look at it?"

"Look?" shouted the stranger. "I want to use it! Do you know how many years it has been since I saw a *seedoor*? GIVE IT TO ME! PLEASE!" The man grabbed it, kissed it, then stood up in his seat and began to shake and shout with fervor! "*BORUCHO ES ADON...*" The entire first class section turned and stared in shock. For the next 10 minutes the man stood and shook wildly as he recited the *Maariv* prayer — word for word without any care or concern for anyone who might be watching. For those 10 minutes he left

Louisiana way below as he ascended to the heavens and the world of his childhood.

With a mixture of great pride and a bit of embarrassment, Steve watched. When the man finished praying, Steve presented the former yeshiva boy with the small *siddur* as a memento because it had evoked such powerful Jewish memories over the Delta.

Perhaps the Torah intentionally called *tefillin* a remembrance. And perhaps, with even more intention, it gave *tefillin* a foreign name. The Torah is telling us that no matter where a Jew may be, whether the jungles of the Congo or the Coptic Islands, Jewish symbols will be there to remind him to come home. As such, Torah observance is not relegated to any specific geographical location. It can be observed, albeit not in toto, every place in the world. For no matter where Jews finds themselves, there are symbols to rekindle their Judaism. They can be derived from everywhere. Even out of Africa.

PARSHAS B'SHALACH

*T*his portion begins with the event that merits the title of the book — Exodus. The Jews were finally sent out from Egypt. Hastily, they gathered their meager possessions, and with the gold and silver that the Egyptians miraculously gave them, they fled.

But one of them, their leader no less, did not take gold and silver. He took Yoseph's bones, and the Torah tells us why. Decades prior, Yoseph had beseeched his children, "*pakod yifkod* — God will surely remember you, and you shall bring my bones up with you out of here" (*Genesis* 50:25).

Slavery can make one forget commitments — especially about old bones. However, despite more than many decades of servitude, Moshe kept the promise. Yet why the wording of the request and its fulfillment? Why did Yoseph juxtapose the words "*pakod yifkod*" (God shall surely remember) with the petition to re-inter his bones? It is also repeated in this portion: "Moshe took the bones of Yoseph with him because Yoseph had adjured the children of Israel saying, *pakod yifkod* — God will surely remember you and you shall bring up my bones from here with you" (*Exodus* 13:19).

It is wonderful that Yoseph assured the nation of its ultimate redemption, but is *that* the reason Moshe took the bones? Didn't he take the bones simply to fulfill a commitment to Yoseph? What does *pakod yifkod* have to do with it? What does the promise of God's remembrance have to do with Moshe's commitment to Yoseph? Why is it inserted in both the request and the response?

Many years ago, our Yeshiva established a Torah audio Torah tape library. As part of my preparations, I looked in the Yellow Pages and found a company that sells tape labels. A very knowledgeable representative took my call. Clearly Jewish, she had a Brooklyn accent and spiced her words with some Yiddish expressions. I felt comfortable dealing with someone whom I believed knew about Jewish institutions. I said I would call her back and asked for her name. She answered proudly, "Esther."

"Last name?" I inquired.

After a brief pause, I received an answer that surprised me. "Scatteregio," she said.

"Scatteregio?" I repeated in amazement. Stepping where perhaps I should not have, I explained my perplexity. "Actually," I offered, "I was expecting Cohen or Goldberg."

She paused, "You are right, I am Jewish and my first husband was Goldman." Another pause. "But now I'm remarried, and it's Scatteregio." She took a deep breath. "But I have a Jewish son, Rick, and he really wants to observe. In fact, he wants me to allow him to study in an Israeli yeshiva."

I knew then that this was not destined to be a telephone call only about tape labels. For half an hour, I talked about the importance of yeshiva, and how Rick could be her link to her past and connection with her future.

I gave her my name and talked about my namesake's influence on an Esther of yesteryear. I ended the conversation with the words "Esther, *es vet zain gut!*" (Yiddish for "it will be well!")

I never knew what kind of impact my words would have.

Ten years later, during the intermediate days of Passover, I took my children to a local park. Many Jewish grandparents were there, watching the next generations slide and swing. An older woman was holding the hand of a young boy who was wearing a large *kipah* and had thick *payos* (sidecurls). As one of my children offered to play with the little boy, I nodded hello and smiled. With pride, she began talking about her children. "Do you know my son Reuvain?" she asked. "He was studying in a Far Rockaway yeshiva until now and just took a job in the city." "Wonderful," I said, "but I don't know your son." She told me about the struggles of making a living, and I had no choice but to listen and smile. Instinctively I responded, "*Es vet zain gut!*" Things will be fine. Her eyes locked on me. She stared in disbelief.

"Mordechai?"

"Esther?"

We just shook our heads in disbelief, and to my amazement, she told me that she was no longer married to Mr. Scattereigo, and that Rick did go to yeshiva, these were his children, and they truly gave her *nachas* (joy).

I will never know if my words helped turn Rick into Reuvain, but I am sure that the words *"es vet zain gut,"* assuring someone that things would be all right, was a statement that stuck longer and faster than any label.

~~~

When Yoseph made his children promise that they would take his bones with them, he added an assurance. He promised them that God would surely remember them. Even Hashem, appearing to Moshe, said, *"pakod pakadti,"* "I have remembered" (*Exodus* 3:16). Yoseph, too, requested to be remembered. Two hundred years of slavery can take an awful toll on people. It can make them give up their pride, it can make them forget about family, it can surely cause them to forget about bones. But when requests are linked with comforting words, they endure. Moshe took Yoseph's bones because they were linked with words of reassurance that remained an anthem of the Jews in exile: "God will remember you." And Moshe remembered, too.

PARSHAS YISRO

He's the Man

arshas Yisro begins by relating how impressed its namesake, Yisro (Jethro), was upon hearing the amazing events that transpired to the nation led by his son-in-law, Moshe. Yisro then decided to convert to Judaism and sent word to Moshe that he would soon be arriving at the Israelite camp. Indeed, Yisro wanted Moshe to leave his post and greet him in the desert before he came to the Israelite camp. The Torah then tells us that Moshe did in fact go out to greet Yisro: "and he bowed and kissed him, and the man asked his dear one about his welfare" (*Exodus* 18:7).

Rashi questions the ambiguity. Who bowed to whom? Who kissed whom? Who was the one to make the gesture? Was it Yisro, the father-in-law, who kissed Moshe, or did Moshe, the son-in-law, leader of millions of people, run to greet his father-in-law, a Midianite priest, and bow and kiss him? Who is the man? Who is the dear one?

Rashi quotes the *Mechilta*, which refers to *Bamidbar* (*Numbers* 12:3) where Moshe is called "the man Moshe." Obviously, then the subject in the verse, "the man bowed and kissed him" in *Parshas* Yisro must mean the one who was referred to as *the man* — Moshe.

Why, however, did the Torah choose a seemingly convoluted way to say that Moshe prostrated himself before his father-in-law? Would it not have been easier to state that "Moshe bowed and kissed him and asked the peace of his dear one?" Why did the Torah use the words "the man" and require us to refer to the *Book of Numbers* to explain who "the man" was? Let the Torah just say Moshe kissed Yisro. Simple!

One time, my brother, Rabbi Zvi Kamenetzky of Chicago, tried to call a friend who was vacationing at Schechter's Caribbean Hotel in Miami Beach, Florida. After about 15 rings, the hotel operator, an elderly, Southern woman who had worked at the hotel for three decades, politely informed my brother that the man was not in his room. "Would you like to leave a message?" she inquired.

"Sure," responded Reb Zvi, "please tell him that Rabbi Kamenetzky called."

The woman at the other end gasped. "Raabbi Kaamenetzky?" she drawled. "Did you say you were Raabbi Kaamenetzky?"

She knew the name! To my brother it sounded as if she were about to follow up with a weighty question. "Yes," he answered. "Why do you ask?"

"Are you," the operator asked, "by any chance related to the famous Raabbi Kaamenetzky?"

There was silence in Chicago. My brother could not imagine that this woman had an inkling of who his grandfather was, the great sage, Dean of Mesivta Torah Voda'ath, to whom thousands had flocked for advice and counsel. She continued. "You know, he passed away about 10 years ago at the end of the wintah?" She definitely had her man, Reb Zvi thought. Still in shock, he offered a subdued, "Yes, I'm his grandson."

"YOOOU ARE?" she exclaimed. "Well, I'm sure glad to talk to ya! Cause your grandpa — he was a real good friend of mine!"

My brother pulled the receiver from his ear and stared at the mouthpiece. He composed himself and slowly began to repeat her words, quizzically. "You say that Rabbi Kamenetzky was a good friend of yours?"

"Sure!" she answered. "Every mornin' Raabbi Kaamenetzky came to this here hotel to teach some sorta Bible class. (It was the *Daf Yomi*.) Now my desk is about 10 yards from the main entrance of the hotel. But every mornin' he made sure to come my way, nod his head, and say 'good mornin' to me. On his way out, he always stopped by my desk and said good-bye. He was a great Rabbi, but he was even a greater man! Oh, yes, he was a wonderful man. He was a real good friend of mine!"

The Torah could have told us the narration in an easier way. It could have told us that Moshe bowed before and kissed Yisro. But the Torah does more. It tells us that it was a *man* who kissed Yisro. True, it was Moshe who performed those actions. But they were not the actions of a Moshe as Moshe our Teacher, they were the actions of Moshe the *mentsch*!

Often, we attribute acts of kindness, compassion, and extra care to the super-human attributes of our sages and leaders. Yet the Torah tells us that it is the simple *mentsch* who performs them. Inside every great leader lies the simple Jew who cares about all people and their feelings. Little wonder, then, that the words "and *the man* Moshe" that Rashi quotes from the *Book of Numbers* begin a verse that fits the explanation quite well. The verse reads, "And *the man* Moshe was exceedingly humble, more than any person on the face of the earth" (*Numbers* 12:3). It was the *man* Moshe who was exceedingly humble, more than any one on the face of the earth.

PARSHAS MISHPATIM

⚘ One Step Back . . . Two Steps Forward

*A*mong the complicated fiduciary matters that this portion discusses, the Torah deals with seemingly simple and mundane issues as well. The Torah discusses donkeys, heavily laden donkeys that belong to your enemy. The Torah tells us, "If you see the donkey of someone you hate crouching beneath its burden, and you refrain from assisting him, you shall repeatedly help him" (*Exodus* 23:5). Obviously, the interjected phrase, "and you refrain from assisting him," begs clarification. After all, if you mustn't refrain from helping him, why mention it in the first place? Rashi explains that the words are to be read rhetorically: "Would you refrain from helping him? How can you let a personal grudge take precedence over the poor animal's pain? Surely you shall continuously help him."

The Talmud in *Bava Metzia* takes the words at face value and explains that there are certain situations where one must refrain from helping unload donkeys. There are other straightforward interpretations as well. But on a simple level, how can we interpret the Torah's strange juxtaposition of our desires to refrain with its command to help?

~

As a youngster, I heard the following story about the great *mussar* luminary, the master ethicist Rabbi Yisrael Lipkin of Salant. Rabbi Lipkin was traveling by train from Salant to Vilna, sitting in the smoking car holding a lit cigar. A young man accosted him, yelling about the putrid odor of the smoke. Other passengers were appalled. After all, they were in the smoking car. Upon hearing the young man, Rabbi Salanter extinguished the cigar and opened the train's window to dissipate the fumes. Only a few seconds later, the young man slammed the window down, screaming at the elderly sage for opening it.

Reb Yisrael apologized profusely to the young man and buried himself in a book of Jewish law.

Upon arriving in Vilna, the young man was horrified to see throngs of people gathered to receive one of Europe's most prominent Rabbis. The young man immediately ran to the home where Rabbi Salanter was staying and began to beg forgiveness. "Don't worry," the sage explained, "a trip can make one edgy. I bear you no ill will. Tell me," the *mussar* master continued, "why did you come to Vilna?"

The young man explained that he was looking to become an ordained *shochet* (slaughterer), and an approbation from a Vilna rabbi would be universally accepted.

Rabbi Lipkin smiled. "My own son-in-law, Reb Elya Lazer, can ordain you. He is a Rav in Vilna. Rest up, and tomorrow you can take the test."

The next day, it was apparent that the young man needed more than rest, for he failed miserably. However, that did not deter Rabbi Lipkin. He encouraged the young man to try again. For the next several weeks, Rabbi Lipkin arranged for tutors and prepared the young man well enough to pass Reb Elya Lazer's make-up exam along with the tests of a host of other well-known Vilna rabbis. Rabbi Lipkin even arranged for the young man to get a job.

Before leaving Vilna, the young man appeared before the *mussar* luminary with tears in his eyes. "Tell me, Rebbe," he cried. "I was able to understand that you could forgive me for my terrible arrogance on the train. But why did you help me so much? That I cannot understand."

Reb Yisrael sat him down, held his hand, and explained. "It is easy to say 'I forgive you.' But deep down, how does one really know if he still bears a grudge? Deep down in my heart I was actually not sure. The only way to remove a grudge is to take action. One who helps another develops a love for the one whom he aided. By helping you, I created a true love which is overwhelmingly more powerful than the words, 'I forgive you.'"

The Torah states that if you see the donkey of your enemy keeling over from its burden, and you want to refrain from helping, know then that that is the time to help. The Torah understands human nature all too well. The sub-conscious speaks very loudly, often telling us to take three steps backwards. But the moment your feet falter is the best time to quicken the forward pace, overpower your emotions, and make a move. It is the time to heal old wounds and close open sores. For overpowering kindness will not only help ease the burdens of a donkey, it will make things a lot lighter for you as well.

PARSHAS TERUMAH

☞ *Job Placement*

*T*he winged seraphs that rest atop the *Aron Kodesh* (Holy Ark) in the Holy of Holies are known as the *cherubim*. These cherubs, the *Midrash* explains, have the faces of innocent children — a young girl and boy. The *Aron Kodesh* contains the most sacred of our physical entities, the *luchos* (Ten Commandments). In the holy sacred box lay both sets of *luchos,* the Tablets that Moshe carved, as well as the shattered pieces of the God-written ones that Moshe smashed upon seeing the Golden Calf. The two cherubs, therefore, sit atop of a lot of history. They also protect a lot of sanctity. Consequently, they must be endowed with singular spiritual symbolism. Yet this is not the first reference to *cherubim* in the Torah. In fact, *cherubim* are mentioned early in creation where they did not sit innocently upon an *Aron Kodesh*. Instead, they stood guard to block Adam and Chava (Eve) from re-entering the Garden of Eden after their expulsion. "Hashem placed the *cherubim* and the flame of the ever-turning sword to guard the path to *Gan Eden*" (*Genesis* 3:24).

The apparent contrast is striking. How is it possible that the very same beings who guard the sanctity, chastity, and purity symbolized by the *Aron Kodesh* could be flashing fiery swords at the gates of Eden? Is a cherub an image of peace, love, and tranquillity, or is it the symbol of destruction and mayhem? It should not represent both — unless the Torah is telling us something. And it is.

※

A rabbi was once speaking to a group of retirees in Miami Beach about the life of the Chofetz Chaim, Rabbi Yisrael Meir HaKohen of Radin. "This great sage," the rabbi explained, "impacted the lives of thousands of Jewish souls with his simple, down-to-earth approach. He published scores of books that applied to everyday living and mastered the art of the parable, imbuing simple tales with profound Jewish concepts."

The rabbi then proceeded to recount a tale that had circulated in the halls of yeshivos the world over. "Once, the Chofetz Chaim was informed that a particular boy in his yeshiva was smoking on *Shabbos*. The *mashgiach* (dean of ethics) of the yeshiva decided that the boy must be ousted from the school. However, the Chofetz Chaim asked to speak to the young man before the expulsion was carried out.

"The young man entered the Chofetz Chaim's study. He was there for only about 15 minutes, and no one knows what the Chofetz Chaim told him, but the story as I heard it," the rabbi exclaimed, "is that not only did the boy decide to remain a *Shabbos* observer for the rest of his life, but he also became a strong supporter of Torah institutions."

The speech ended, and the crowd shuffled out. But one elderly man remained fixed in his chair, his face ashen and his eyes focused directly at the rabbi. Slowly, the man got up and approached the lectern. "Where did you hear that story?" he demanded. "Do you know who that boy was?"

The rabbi shook his head nervously. "No," he stammered, not imagining where the conversation was leading.

"It was me!" the old man cried. "And do you know what the Chofetz Chaim told me?"

Again the rabbi, not knowing what to say, shook his head. "I have no idea," he said. "Honestly, I have no idea. What did the Chofetz Chaim say?"

The elderly man smiled. "The Chofetz Chaim said absolutely nothing." As his mind raced back more than half a century, the old man repeated the words again. "Absolutely nothing. He just held my hand — the one that held the cigarettes — and began to cry. Then the Chofetz Chaim slowly began to whisper the words 'Shabbos, Shabbos' over and over in a sad singsong. And his tears slowly dripped on my hand that had held a cigarette just hours earlier.

"He sat there without looking at me," the man continued. "Crying. He felt the pain of *Shabbos* desecration. And I felt his pain, too. Just being there with him for those 15 minutes changed the hand that held the cigarette into the hand that would hold up the Torah."

Rav Yaakov Kamenetzky, of blessed memory, used to comment that the *cherubim* who held swords as they stood guard at the gates of Eden are not doomed to remain in that position. Young children are affected by their whereabouts and can change greatly when they are placed in different situations. Place them as a guard and they will brandish swords. But when they are on top of the *Aron*, they will cherish it. Put them with the *Aron Kodesh* — let them feel its sanctity — and they will become the *cherubim* we aspire to emulate.

PARSHAS TEZAVEH

～ Case Clothed

"Clothes," the adage goes, "make the man." But did you ever wonder about the man who makes the clothes? This week's portion discusses the priestly vestments worn by both the common *kohen* (priest) and the *Kohen Gadol* (High Priest). The common *kohen* wore four simple garments while the *Kohen Gadol* wore eight ornate and complex garments, including a jewel-studded breastplate, a honeycomb-woven tunic, an apron-like robe, and a specially designed coat adorned with gold bells and woven pomegranates. Highly skilled artisans were necessary to embroider and fashion them.

Indeed, weaving such garments was quite a complex task, and Moshe had to direct the craftsmen about the particularly difficult sartorial laws. Yet when Hashem charged Moshe, He described the function of the garments much differently than He did when telling Moshe what to command the tailors.

Moshe was told by Hashem to "make holy vestments for Ahron for glory and splendor" (*Exodus* 28:2). That description is surely wonderful, but glory and splendor are very physical attributes. Yet when Moshe was told to command the artisans, the message he was told to impart was quite different. "You shall speak to the wise-hearted people whom I have invested with a spirit of wisdom, as they shall make Ahron's vestments to sanctify him and minister to Me" (*Exodus* 28:1-3). "The clothes," Moshe told the tailors, "were not meant for glory or splendor; they were to sanctify and to minister." Why the change in stated purpose?

～～

My brother-in-law, Rabbi Simcha Lefkowitz,

Rabbi of Congregation Toras Chaim of Hewlett, New York, attended a *taharah* (ritual ceremony to prepare a deceased Jew for burial) for an individual whose background was rooted in a Chasidic community. The members of the *Chevra Kadisha* (burial society) are often immune to the emotions, trauma, and dread that would normally accompany such preparations. It therefore did not strike the rabbi as odd that the *Chevra* members did their job with hardly a word spoken or an emotional gesture. Years of working with the departed can numb the senses of even the toughest men.

All of a sudden, however, a murmur bounced back and forth between members of the *Chevra*. "*Er hut a visa?*" (He has a visa?) they queried. Then the conversation took a stranger turn. They began to mumble about a first-class ticket.

The rabbi became concerned. Why was anyone talking about travel plans during this most sacred of rituals? It could be that the burial was to take place in Israel, but he was sure that a dead man needed no visa. The entire conversation just did not make sense.

Immediately, the room became silent, filled with a sense of awe and reverence. "*Er hut a visa!*" exclaimed the senior member of the group. The entire *Chevra* nodded and the atmosphere suddenly changed.

While they continued to prepare for the funeral, it was as if the deceased had been a great sage or Chasidic Rebbe. Yet, Rabbi Lefkowitz was unable to understand the different attitude until the eldest man beckoned him. "Come here," he said. "I'll show you something." The old man lifted the arm of the deceased to reveal seven numbers crudely tattooed on his forearm. "Do you know what they are?"

"Of course," Rabbi Lefkowitz replied. "They are the numbers that the Nazis tattooed on prisoners in the concentration camps."

"No," the old man said. "These numbers are a first-class ticket to *Gan Eden*. They are the visa, and they are the tickets. Period."

The badges we wear have different meanings for every individual. Moshe, the man of God who saw the world with a profound vision of spirituality, was told about the more mundane aspect of the priestly garments. "They are for glory and splendor." But he is told to charge the artisans, who often see only the splendor and glory of the physical world, with the true purpose of the garments — "to sanctify and minister."

Often, we see numbers, events, and even garments as the mere manifestation of natural events which impart in us only a sense of awe for the history or beauty within. Sometimes, we mortals must be reminded of a sense even greater than glory and splendor — ministration and sanctification of God's name.

PARSHAS KI SISA

➣ *To See or Not to See*

*D*uring the Temple era, Jews traveled to Jerusalem three times a year for the major festivals. It was an exhilarating experience: the entire Jewish nation ascended upon the city's beautiful hills, took part in the services at the Holy Temple, and relished the splendor and spirituality. Of necessity, the scene influenced their lives — surely until the next holiday. Today, even with the Temple destroyed, throngs of visitors flock to its ancient walls, coming to see its beauty and ponder days of old. They imagine themselves as pilgrims of years past traveling to Jerusalem as God commands in the Torah.

The only problem is that He never told us to come and see Jerusalem. In fact, the Torah tells us quite the opposite.

"Three times a year all your males shall appear (in Jerusalem) before the Lord Hashem, the God of Israel" (*Exodus* 34:23).

Why is the command given in that manner? Can't God see us wherever we are? Isn't the trip to Jerusalem to see the sights, and hear the sounds, and experience the splendor? Are we not going to see Jerusalem rather than be seen there?

⚜

Not so long ago I was in the Newark Airport early in the morning. Before heading back home, I decided to purchase a cup of black coffee at one of the many stands in airport environs.

Walking toward the cafe, I noticed a bearded man wearing a cardigan sweater. While he looked like a true academic, something else he was wearing made him appear noticeably different. A large knit *yarmulke* sat comfortably on his head, so large, in fact, that it looked more like a beret than a *kipah*.

He sat at a table near the coffee bar, eating a pastry and sipping coffee. As one who enjoys *shmoozing* with Jews of all varieties and walks of life, I noted to myself that after I made my purchase I would say *shalom* to him. Steaming black coffee in hand, I walked toward his table and I was startled to see the man sitting there coffee in hand, half-eaten pastry on the table, but *sans yarmulke*.

Thoroughly confused, I wrinkled my brow and approached his table. "Excuse me," I asked, politely and very carefully. While my next question would probably be an invasion of his privacy, my curiosity got the better of my manners. After introducing myself, and asking his name, I asked the rude question. "Weren't you just wearing a *kipah*?"

He just smiled. "Yes."

"I thought so," I meekly responded. "Pray tell me," I continued, as politely as I could, "did you take it off after seeing me?" Again he nodded. "Yes."

Suddenly pangs of guilt encompassed me. After all, in a small way I felt that my job is to get people to put on a *yarmulke*, not take one off! "What made you take off your *kipah*?" I asked.

"I'll explain," he began. "When you walked by, I was eating a pastry that I purchased from the cafe. You see, I just began observing kosher, and the letter of kosher certification taped near the display was good enough for my standard today.

"However, by wearing a *yarmulke* while eating, I felt that I declared this food as certified kosher by *yarmulke* standards. You," he said, pointing towards me, "obviously an Orthodox Jew, walked by. You may have noticed my attire, and my food, and assumed that I endorsed it at a higher level. I did not want you to purchase the pastry because of me. So I took off my *yarmulke*. Simple as that!"

✦

We go to Israel for many reasons: family, friends, business.

But no matter what our stated motives are, everybody goes to see the country. Three times a year the Torah commands us to go up to Jerusalem. Of course, there is much to see there that will inspire us: the Temple Mount, the priests, the Holy City. Today, even without the Temple, there is much to inspire us: the Western Wall, the hundreds of Torah institutions that dot the city and lend flavor to its ancient landscape, the many people. But in this portion the Torah tells us that when we go to Jerusalem we are there for a twofold purpose. We stand in Hashem's court-yard, but we are not there to watch. Rabbi Mordechai Gifter of Telshe Yeshiva says that people think Israel is a museum! It's not. Israel and Jerusalem are not there to be observed and critiqued. When we go there, it is *we* who are watched, critiqued and cher-ished by the Observer of all His handiwork. We are not going to watch, we are going to *be* watched, too — by God.

PARSHAS VAYAKHEL

Focal Points

*T*he commands for building the *Mishkan* (traveling Tabernacle) were fully dispensed . As the job was winding down, in *Parshas Vayakhel* Moshe gave the nation the final directives of the monumental task. First, however, he had a message. The portion begins by telling us that Moshe gathered the nation and told them that "Six days work may be done, and the seventh day shall be holy . . . you shall not kindle fire in any of your dwellings on the Sabbath day" (*Exodus* 35:2-3). Only then does he continue with the directives that pertain to the completion of the *Mishkan*.

The strange juxtaposition of the laws of *Shabbos* in the midst of the instructions about building the Sanctuary is confusing. Our sages explain that Moshe was informing the Jewish people that despite the *Mishkan*'s importance, building it does not preempt the Sabbath. Indeed, all work must cease on *Shabbos* regardless of its impact on the progress of the *Mishkan*.

However, why the seemingly disconnected verses? Why didn't the Torah tell us of *Shabbos*' requirements in a straightforward way, by openly directing the nation "You shall not construct the *Mishkan* on the *Shabbos*"? Why juxtapose *Shabbos* as a separate unit, leaving us to infer its overriding power through Scriptural juxtaposition? In fact, the words "You shall not kindle fire in any of your dwellings on the Sabbath" make the command seem totally irrelevant to the *Mishkan* per se and applicable instead only to every individual homemaker. If so, the command is out of place. Yet, regardless of its relation to the laws of daily life, *Shabbos* plays a greater role vis-à-vis the *Mishkan*. What is it?

A famous *maggid* (storyteller) was asked to speak in a synagogue in a prosperous and modern city. Yet, before he was allowed to speak he was sent to consult with the synagogue president. "This is a very distinguished community," the *maggid* was told "and we must be careful. We surely would not want to offend anyone with even the slightest rebuke."

The *maggid* went to meet the president, who was sitting in a richly upholstered leather armchair behind a mahogany desk. As the *maggid* entered, the man rested his lit cigar on the corner of a brass ashtray.

"Rabbi," said the president, "you have a reputation as a remarkable speaker, one who inspires crowds and makes — might I say — waves. Pray tell me," he asked "what are you intending to speak about in our town?"

The *maggid* promptly replied, "I intend to talk about *Shabbos* observance."

The president's face turned crimson. "Oh no, dear rabbi, please. In this town, such talk will fall on deaf ears. We all struggle to make a living, and *Shabbos* is just not in the cards. I implore you, talk about something else."

The *maggid* pondered. "Perhaps I should talk about *kashrut*."

"*Kashrut*? Please," begged the president, "don't waste your time. There hasn't been a kosher butcher in this town for years."

"How about *tzedaka*?" offered the *maggid*.

"Charity?" the president said, horrified. "Give us a break. Do you know how many *shnorrers* (collectors) visit this town each week? We are sick of hearing about charity!"

Meekly the *maggid* made another suggestion. "*Tefillah*?"

"Please," the president cried, "in a city of 1,000 Jewish families, we hardly get a weekday *minyan* (quorum for prayer). The synagogue is empty, except on the High Holy Days. No one is interested."

Finally, the *maggid* became frustrated. "If I can't

talk about *Shabbos*, and I can't talk about *tzedaka*, and I cannot discuss *kashrut* or prayer, what do you want me to talk about?"

The president looked amazed. "Why, rabbi," exclaimed the president, "that's easy! Talk about Judaism!"

By placing the concept of *Shabbos* in general, and one of its most detailed laws in particular, right smack in the middle of the architectural directives concerning a most glorious edifice, the Torah is telling us that although we may build beautiful palaces in which to serve the Almighty, if we forget the tenets of our faith, then that great structure is meaningless. *Shabbos* was mentioned as a separate unit because its relevance is even greater than its ability to halt construction. A Jew must remember that without *Shabbos*, without *kashrut*, without *tefillah*, a beautiful sanctuary is no more enduring than a castle in the air.

PARSHAS PEKUDEI

✐ Unlimited Partnership

*T*he *Mishkan* (traveling Tabernacle) was finally complete. As the nation looked at the magnificent work with great joy, Moshe was proud. So proud, in fact, that he did something that he did only once again, just before his death: he blessed the entire nation.

Actually, the erection of a *Mishkan* in itself was the greatest blessing, for Hashem had promised the Jewish nation in *Parshas Terumah,* "They shall build Me a *Mishkan* — and I will dwell among them" (*Exodus* 25:8). But Moshe felt that he, too, would add his own blessing.

Rashi (*Exodus* 39:43) explains that Moshe told the people: "May Hashem rest His presence in your handiwork."

At first, it seems that Moshe is merely reiterating the promise that Hashem Himself had made. Hashem had promised to dwell in the midst of the Sanctuary that the Jewish nation would build. Why, then, did Moshe repeat God's promise as a blessing? Was he beseeching Hashem to keep His word? Or was he perhaps bestowing a more powerful message to the nation?

※

A man once approached Rabbi Yehuda Assad for advice. "There is an old, run-down store in the downtown area of the city," the man said. "I can get it for a very reasonable price. I think that with my marketing skills I may be able to turn that location into a profitable venture. Do you think I should buy it?"

Rabbi Assad made a face. "I don't think that it would be prudent to enter that part of the city for a business venture."

The man left, somewhat dejected.

A few days later another man entered the rabbi's study with the identical question about the same property. "There is an old, run-down store in the downtown area of the city. I can get it for a very reasonable price. I think that with my marketing skills, and of course with Hashem's help, I may be able to turn that location into a profitable venture. Do you think I should buy it?"

This time Rabbi Assad nodded his approval. "I think you could make a go of it. I have no doubts that it will be a success."

When word got out that the rabbi was behind this new endeavor, the first man stormed into Rabbi Assad's study quite upset. "Why did you tell me not to buy the property and then tell my friend just the opposite?" he demanded.

"My dear friend," the rabbi answered, "there is a great difference. Your friend took in a partner. He said that with the help of Hashem he could make a go of it. When someone includes Hashem in his plans, I am sure that he will succeed!"

For the first time since the Exodus, the Jews had become accomplished craftsmen, artisans, tailors, and contractors. They built a magnificent edifice in the wilderness. Moshe knew that a feeling of self-gratification might naturally accompany their accomplishments. Perhaps they might even begin to think that it was *their* wisdom, *their* skills, and *their* abilities alone that made the beautiful *Mishkan* possible. So he blessed them with words that were meant to dissuade any such delusion.

"May Hashem's presence rest in your handiwork." Of course, Hashem promised that He would dwell in the *Mishkan*. Moshe's unspoken question was, "Would the Jews let Him in? Would they make Him a partner? Would they recognize Hashem as a significant factor even in the physical handiwork that they themselves had wrought?"

To that end, Moshe's blessing incorporated the standard for every action, accomplishment, and success that anyone achieves. May Hashem be a part of your success. May the *Shechina* (Holy Spirit of Hashem) rest within your handiwork.

ספר ויקרא

The Book of
Leviticus

PARSHAS VAYIKRA

⌐ *Give It While It's Hot*

*I*n this *parsha*, the Torah tells us of a *mitzvah* that the Chofetz Chaim is alleged to have prayed that he never would have to perform. Yet, difficult as it may be, it is a positive commandment. But as the Chofetz Chaim wished, may we all be spared from it!

The Torah states that if an individual succumbed and stole property, or deceitfully held an item entrusted to him, it is a *mitzvah* to make amends. "And he shall return the stolen object that he stole, the fraudulent gains that he defrauded or the pledge that was secured with him . . ." (*Leviticus* 5:23). The redundancy is glaring. Of course, the stolen item is what the person stole. Surely the pledge was secured with the thief. And the fraudulent gains are those that were swindled. Why does the Torah repeat the words, "that he stole, that he defrauded, that was secured with him"?

From the extra words the Talmud derives the technical laws that determine when monetary restitution takes precedence over reparations of the stolen object itself. If a person steals a piece of wood, for example, and builds a boat with it, must he return the newly formed item to the original owner of the wood, or will monetary compensation suffice? After all, the wood in the thief's possession is no longer "the stolen object that he stole." The man stole wood; it is now a boat. On such issues there is much analysis written over the centuries. Yet, the seeming redundancies can also be explained on a simple, homiletic level.

⌐⌐⌐

**Rabbi Moshe Sofer, beloved Rabbi of Pressburg
and author of the noted work *Chasam Sofer*, once sold**

his silver candlesticks in order to lend someone a large sum of money. A few days after the loan was repaid, he received a package containing a beautiful sterling *kiddush* cup. That Friday night the *Chasam Sofer* took the cup out of its velvet pouch and raised it for his entire family to see.

"Look how beautiful this *becher* (goblet) is," he declared. "Do you notice the intricate etchings? It must be worth a fortune!"

The family looked on in horror. They knew that the gift had been sent by the one who borrowed the money. And that was a form of interest, prohibited by the Torah. They could not begin to imagine why the *Chasam Sofer* had removed it and was seemingly admiring it. Abruptly, the *Chasam Sofer* stopped talking. His eyes became focused sternly on the cup. Once again, he began to speak. "But, my children, the Torah tells us we may not take interest! Therefore, I will put this beautiful cup away and never use it. In fact, it must be returned to the sender immediately, and he must be told of the prohibition."

Then the *Chasam Sofer* continued. "You must be wondering why I even looked at the cup. You certainly must be bewildered why I admired it openly. I will explain. How often is it that I am offered interest? Never! Since people do not approach me for loans, I have never felt the passion or desire to accept interest. Now, when I have the opportunity to observe the Torah's prohibition, I want to make sure that I do so from a vantage of passion. I want to realize what I am turning down. I want to value the Torah's command specifically as it applies to an exquisite and ornate silver goblet. And so, I feel that by working up our desire for the item we surely would appreciate its refusal."

Perhaps the Torah is hinting at the most proper aspect of restitution. There are two reasons to return a stolen item. First, a person is in possession of an item that is not his. Simple. But there is another reason. Every one of our actions helps mold us.

By returning an item that we once desired enough to have stolen, we train ourselves to overcome our covetous constitution. We learn that even though we want something, we may not take it. And if we do take it, we *must* return it.

How much more effective is restitution when the desire for the item still exists. After all, a stolen item that one may have forgotten about, or lost desire for, is much easier to return. Ten years after you stole a bicycle you probably would be driving a car, so the desire for the bike is no longer there. That is why Maimonides teaches us that the greatest act of *teshuva* (repentance) occurs when the passion for the crime still exists. While repentance is always accepted, if the item is still in your mind as "the stolen item that you stole, the fraudulent gains that you defrauded, the pledge that was secured with you," then repentance is so much more meaningful.

When desires conflict with conscience — and conscience prevails — that is true *teshuva*. Fifty years after a crime, there are those who may issue apologies and excuses. However, a lingering question remains: are they "stolen items that you stole," or are they just black-and-white memories of an almost-forgotten crime? The words "I am sorry" should not be merely a sorry excuse, but rather an expression of true regret coupled with a sincere commitment never to sin again. And that can best happen while the iron (or steal) is still hot.

PARSHAS TZAV

✐ Pure Confusion

As the laws of the *korbonos* (sacrifices) are explicated through the ensuing Torah portions, more and more complex issues arise dealing with seemingly esoteric spirituality. While the concept of animal sacrifice may be difficult for modern people to comprehend, the sages of yore, including Maimonides and Nachmanides, dealt comfortably and in great detail with their concepts, rationale, and purpose.

In this *parsha*, in addition to defining the various laws that distinguish different types of sacrifices, the Torah presents the concepts of *tumah* and *taharah*, loosely translated as spiritual impurity and purity. Of course, these laws have nothing to do with sanitary conditions; rather, the laws define a state of spirituality that changes with life and death. Specifically, the Torah states that any meat of a sacrifice that contacts anything *tamei* (impure) shall not be eaten.

Simply stated, the law is that when *tahor* meets *tamei*, pure meets impure, *tamei* prevails and lowers the *tahor* to a state of *tamei*. The Kotzker Rebbe, Rabbi Menachem Mendel Morgenstern, is concerned: why so? Why does *tumah* depreciate *taharah*? Why not the opposite? When purity meets impurity, should it not automatically purify it? Let the impure become elevated by contact with purity.

~~~

Rabbi Shaul Kagan, of blessed memory, was the *Rosh Kollel* (Dean) of Kollel Bais Yitzchok in Pittsburgh, PA. In addition to being a brilliant Talmudic scholar, he was very witty. As a member of

the *Kollel*, I was a student of his, and he once related the following story to me:

Back in the early 1940s, when mental disability was not well understood, a man was committed to an insane asylum due to his aberrant behavior. After months of treatment, the doctors felt that he was cured and allowed him to leave. The man, however, refused to go. "I will not leave this institution unless you sign a document stating that I am sane," he declared. Since the doctors had given him a clean bill of mental health, they figured they might as well acquiesce to his strange demand.

Not long after his release, the man went for a job interview. After answering the questions quite impressively, the man leaned toward his prospective boss and asked in earnest, "Now that you asked me about myself, may I ask you a question?"

The interviewer replied, "Certainly!"

"Mister," the former mentally ill patient began, "are you normal?"

The man was a little taken aback but replied, "I surely think so. Why do you ask?"

"You see, mister," the applicant declared while proudly displaying his signed document, "you only think that you are normal. I, however, have a certificate!"

The Kotzker Rebbe explains that when it comes to the world of pure and impure, there are facts we know for certain, and there are particulars of which we can never be sure. The world of purity, unfortunately, is not as absolute as the world of impurity. We may think something is actually pure; we may assume that it is untouched and untampered. However, we may never know the truth: we do not know its history, where it went, what it touched, or what affected it. We are shocked and horrified at the terrible deeds of youngsters who were deemed innocent and pure, or of leaders who were supposed to guide us to the moral high ground. We may have thought they were *tahor*. Unfortunately, however, what we may think is pure, innocent, and holy is sometimes not.

Tumah, on the other hand, is well defined. We know with certainty what is not pure and holy. It has a certificate. Therefore, the Kotzker Rebbe explains, when bona-fide *tumah* attaches to something that is at best hopefully and assumedly pure, definite impurity prevails and defiles that which was assumed *tahor*.

For example, when asked if an item is kosher, I have heard others reply, "I know that it is under supervision. I certainly hope that it is kosher!"

In a world of mixed messages and confusing signals, we can try to cling to perceived purity. And we can hope and pray that the role models and values that we have chosen are the correct ones.

But we must surely keep away from those ideas and actions that are clearly defined as impure. Such deeds can leave an impact powerful enough to taint the purest *neshamos* (souls). We *can* avoid them. After all, they have a certificate!

PARSHAS SHMINI

↗ *Hairline Fractures*

ormally, the righteous prevail. Noach is saved from the flood, while the evil generation drowns. Avraham defeats the four evil kings and rescues his nephew Lot. Yaakov outwits his conniving Uncle Lavan. The Jews escape Egypt and leave their pursuers submerged in the Red Sea. Yes, *tzadikim* always seem to triumph.

Except in *Parshas Shmini*, which depicts the opening day of the newly dedicated *Mishkan* (Tabernacle) in all its grandeur.

Ahron was servicing, the Levites were singing, and Moshe was coordinating. Then tragedy struck. Two of Ahron's sons, Nadav and Avihu, offered an *aish zarah*, a strange fire, to Hashem, something defined as an unauthorized offering brought without consulting either their father or Moshe. Nadav and Avihu were punished by a fire emanating from the Holy of Holies which consumed them. The celebration was tragically marred. Ahron was dumbstruck. And Moshe had to put back all the pieces.

Moshe declared to Ahron, "This is what Hashem spoke, 'from my nearest I shall be sanctified . . . ' And Ahron was silent" (*Leviticus* 10:3). While Moshe declared to an entire nation that these two men were considered the dearest and nearest to Hashem, their undertaking, however, did not pass God's scrutiny, and they perished. It does not seem fair.

Indeed, every time a righteous man passes, or tragedy strikes a seemingly upstanding family, we are all left speechless. Why do what we consider bad things happen to those we consider good people? I don't intend to give a complete answer: unlike some popular authors, I don't claim to have it. But I'd like to share some thoughts based on this episode.

Years ago, America was shocked into national mourning. The Challenger Space Shuttle exploded into a molten mass of steel and silicon as we lost six of America's finest and one of our own extended family. My son asked me, "why?"

My son and I were not the only ones bothered with the question. Millions of dollars were spent to find the physical evidence. There were mountains of documents and hundreds of researchers all shared the questions that little children across the world asked along with presidents, princes, and noblemen — why? After three months of intensive investigation NASA came up with an answer. There was a microscopic hairline fracture in an o-ring seal. A microscopic fissure destroyed the lives of seven astronauts, sent a country into mourning, and threw a multi-billion dollar space program into chaos. Explain that to a seven-year-old! For years his toy train set has been running with cracks the size of a seismic fault, yet a massive space shuttle exploded because of a hairline fracture. It was difficult for me to explain it, but my son helped me out.

"I guess, Aba," he pondered, "that when you are in a rocket ship, the little cracks count more."

The Torah teaches a fascinating lesson. The more dear one is to Hashem, the more lethal the hairline fractures.

Despite the greatness of Nadav and Avihu, young leaders who saw the word of Hashem in every one of their father's movements, they could not of their own volition initiate a new offering or service in the Holy of Holies. It may seem to be a small sin, a hairline fracture in our eyes, but when dealing with something as enormous as Hashem's desires, it is unfortunately deadly.

Rabbi Eliyahu Lopian was asked about the stringency of writing *tefillin*: if even one letter is split or cracked, the *tefillin* are invalid. "Rebbe," a young man asked, "one crack in one letter and an $800 pair of tefillin is *posul*?"

Reb Elya, as he was affectionately known, walked over to a transistor radio, he opened the back panel, and showed the young man the array of hair-thin circuits. "Cut one of these," the sage said, "and what have you got? Nothing!"

The world of spirituality is as delicate and precise as the most complex computer board. It is as volatile as an atomic bomb. The higher one's level, the closer he is to his Creator, the more scrutinized he is, the more severe is Hashem's judgment. We are often judged with great leniency — our cracks don't affect our performance. Yet there are much greater men and women who are as important and delicate as the most complex creations. And it is through those dear ones that Hashem's presence is felt.

PARSHAS TAZRIA

➤ Kohen . . . Kohen . . . Gone

arshas Tazria deals predominantly with the physio-spiritual plague that affects gossipers and rumor mongers — *tzora'as*. *Tzora'as* appears as a white lesion on the body, and the status of the afflicted person depends on the lesion's shade of white, its size, and development. Someone afflicted with *tzora'as* does not go to a medical clinic to seek treatment, nor does he enter a hospital. Instead he is quarantined and then re-evaluated; if he is judged to have a severe case, he is sent out of the Jewish camp until he heals, the latter a sign that he has repented his slanderous ways. No physician or medical expert evaluates him; instead, an afflicted person is evaluated, re-evaluated, and has his future determined by none other than a *kohen* (priest). Moreover, the Torah does not keep that detail a secret. In the 47 verses that discuss the bodily affliction of *tzora'as*, the *kohen* is mentioned no less than 45 times! "He shall be brought to the *kohen*," "the *kohen* shall look," "the *kohen* shall declare him contaminated," "the *kohen* shall quarantine him," "the *kohen* shall declare him *tahor* (pure) . . . " (*Leviticus* 13:1-47).

Why must the Torah include the *kohen*'s involvement in every aspect of the process? Moreover, why does the Torah mention the *kohen*'s involvement in virtually every verse? Would it not have been sufficient to have one encompassing edict: "The entire process is supervised and executed according to the judgment of the *kohen*"?

➤➤

The parents of a developmentally disabled child entered the study of Rabbi Shlomo Zalman Auerbach. They had decided to place their child in a special

school where he would also live; the question was which one.

"Have you asked the boy where he would like to go?" the sage asked. The parents were dumbfounded.

"Our child cannot be involved in the process! He hasn't the capacity to understand," the father explained.

Rabbi Auerbach was not moved, "You are sinning against your child. You are removing him from his home, placing him in a foreign environment, and you don't even consult the child? He will feel helpless and betrayed. I'd like to talk to him."

The couple quickly went home and brought the boy to the Torah sage.

"My name is Shlomo Zalman," the venerable scholar smiled. "What's yours?"

"Akiva."

"Akiva," Rabbi Auerbach explained, "I am one of the leading Torah sages in the world, and many people discuss their problems with me. Now I need your help. You are about to enter a special school, and I need a representative to look after all the religious matters in the school. I would like to give you *smicha* (ordination), making you my official rabbinical representative. You can freely discuss any issue with me whenever you want."

Rabbi Auerbach then gave the boy a warm handshake and a hug.

The boy moved into the school and flourished. In fact, due to his great sense of responsibility, he rarely wanted to leave school, even for a weekend; after all, who would take care of any questions that would arise?

⋘

Part of the *metzora's* (afflicted person's) healing process is banishment from the Jewish camp. However, it is a delicate ordeal, one wrought with trauma, pain, and emotional distress. The *kohen*, a man of peace, love, and compassion, must be there for every part of the process; he must be there to guide the *metzora* through the tension-filled incubation period as well as his discharge from the camp. Moreover, the *kohen* is there again to ease the *metzora* back into society.

By constantly repeating the word *kohen* the Torah reiterates that every traumatic decision needs spiritual guidance. Even an ostensibly cold-hearted punishment can be transformed into a process of spiritual redemption! A tough, seemingly dispassionate decision can be made into a beautiful experience. For when the *kohen* holds a person's hand, even if it is a stricken one, even if he is leading a *metzora* outside the camp, away from the community, he is definitely not gone and certainly not forgotten.

Parshas
Metzora

⟫ *Strange Altar-Fellows*

arshas Metzora deals with the purification process of the person afflicted with *tzora'as* (a leprosy-like affliction). After the disease heals, the formerly afflicted person is instructed to bring a sacrifice that includes two very different items.

"And he shall take two live, clean birds, cedarwood, crimson thread, and hyssop" (*Leviticus* 14:4). The Torah details the offering and all of its intricacies, leaving the commentaries to ponder the symbolism of combining wood from the tallest tree with the lowly hyssop moss.

Rashi explains that "the hyssop symbolizes the humility that the *metzora* should have, while the cedar is a symbolic reminder that he who holds himself as high as the cedar tree should learn to lower himself like the hyssop."

Wouldn't the hyssop alone teach or symbolize humility? What point is there in bringing cedar as well? Further, if bringing moss represents the need for humility, couldn't the cedar offering represent the need for pride? There is however, another explanation for joining the two.

———

A few years after Rabbi Shneur Kotler succeeded his late father, Rabbi Ahron Kotler, as the *Rosh Yeshiva* (Dean) of the Lakewood Yeshiva, the Yeshiva's enrollment began to expand. As such, Reb Shneur was no longer able to sit and study in the large study hall all day. Suddenly, he was forced to raise funds all day, often leaving early in the morning and returning home past midnight.

The annual convention of Agudath Israel was a brief respite, where nearly 1,000 laymen and rabbinical leaders gathered for a long weekend to discuss the state of Torah affairs.

My grandfather, Rabbi Yaakov Kamenetzky, the senior member of the Council of Torah Sages, often highlighted the keynote session on Saturday night. As the eldest of the world's acknowledged Torah sages, Reb Yaakov would find a way to sneak up to the dais, usually through a back door, to avoid having the entire crowd arise upon seeing him — an honor required by Jewish law. Yet that year things were different. Reb Yaakov engaged the much younger Reb Shneur in conversation outside the large ballroom and waited until everyone took his seat. Then he took Reb Shneur by the hand and said, "I think it is time we took our seats, too." He proudly held Reb Shneur by the arm and escorted him to the dais as the throng of people rose in awe.

Reb Shneur, stunned by Reb Yaakov's departure from his trademark humility, asked him why he did not enter through the back of the hall as was his usual custom.

"Reb Shneur," my grandfather explained, "your *rebbitzen* (rabbi's wife) is sitting in the women's section. The entire year she sees you in a much-dishonored light. You run from donor to donor in order to keep the yeshiva open, you have hardly any time to prepare your lectures, and you have people knocking on your door at all hours with their problems. Yet she stands beside you, faithful and unwavering. It is time that she see you get a little *kavod* (honor)."

~~~

Rabbi Yitzchak Meir of Gur explains that sometimes people become so humble that they can achieve wonderful accomplishments. Indeed, humility can also breed self-effacement that may lead to despair. Of course, Rashi is correct in explaining that one who is as haughty as the cedar must humble himself like the lowly moss. But one must also bear in mind an equally important fact — at times, after one has been humiliated as low as the hyssop, he must rise in his own eyes to the height of a cedar and proudly exclaim that he can and will accomplish the lofty goals to which he legitimately aspires. And those are goals that only the cedar's limbs can attain.

So the lowly hyssop must be bound with a seemingly mis-matched counterpart, the cedar. Because when they are offered hand-in-hand, they have a lot to learn from each other.

PARSHAS ACHAREI MOS

✏ *Home Rule*

*C*hukim are laws that have no rational explanation. They are directives from the Almighty, and our observance of them is testimony to our constant and unconditional commitment to His every desire.

That is why it is difficult to understand the juxtaposition of two verses mentioning *chukim*. "Do not perform the practices of Egypt where you have dwelled, or the practices of Canaan where I bring you, and in their *chukim* (customs) do not follow. [However,] you shall perform My laws and safeguard My *chukim* (decrees)" (*Leviticus* 18:3-4).

The Torah's *chukim* are hard enough to follow. So why would anyone follow the unexplainable customs and decrees practiced by non-Jews? Those Jews who find themselves driven by seemingly rational thought and reason often scoff at the complexities of decrees that transcend the human mind. Surely, they would not fall prey to follow blindly the strange whims of idol worshippers or cults. Or would they?

❦

As a student in the Philadelphia Yeshiva, I heard a story that was probably as apocryphal as it was amusing. A Talmudic scholar was travelling by train from Philadelphia to Harrisburg. The man had a beard, long dark coat, and large wide-brimmed black hat. After placing his bags over his seat, he sat down next to a well-groomed businessman who looked at him scornfully. For the first 20 minutes of the trip, the secular gentleman kept eyeing the student as if he wanted to tell him something.

Finally, the businessman could no longer contain himself. With passion in his voice, the man began to shout, "You know, I'm sick and tired of Jews who think they are still in the Middle Ages! You are a disgrace! I'm Jewish, too. I even speak Yiddish. But do I wear a black coat? Do I let my beard grow? Must I wear an oversized hat? No! Why do you wear those clothes? Why do you wear that beard? Why do you need that hat? It's time you woke up and joined the modern world — the world of America!"

The startled student looked at his accuser quizzically. In a perfect Pennsylvanian accent, he began to speak.

"Jewish?" he queried. "Excuse me, sir, I'm Amish, and I'm on my way back home from a visit with relatives in Philadelphia. I am sorry if I offend you with my style of dress, but this is part of our heritage and culture. It was passed from our families in Europe to our families here in Lancaster. I am sorry if I have disturbed you."

The businessman's face turned ashen. "I'm awfully sorry," he said contritely, "I did not mean what I said. In fact, I think it is wonderful that you maintain your heritage, culture, and tradition with such enthusiasm. It shows courage, fortitude, and commitment. Please forgive me. I was truly insensitive."

Suddenly a wide smile broke across the young man's face. In perfect Yiddish he asked the reeling traveler one simple question. "For the gentile it's wonderful, but for the Jew it's a disgrace?"

❦

Sadly, *mitzvos* that are difficult to understand often discourage Jews who have not had a total Torah experience. Those *mitzvos* become the scapegoat for a lack of adherence to even simple and very comprehensible commands. Yet many of those same intellectuals struggle to understand the culture, customs, and unexplainable rituals of both the society they live in and, in many instances, distant cultures. I have met scholars who have studied the sociological nuances of Zulu tribes, but have never devoted more than an elementary level of study to their own heritage. While such misplaced sensitivity is undoubtedly due to the inherent respect that Jews have for all humans, there still must be a balance. One can study arcane gentile sartorial customs — even *chukim* — with awe and admiration if their fulfillment sits on top of a non-Jew's head. Yet the same person would never give any thought to the meaning of a beard and *payos* that may adorn a Jewish skull. Thousands of unaffiliated college students who buy recordings of Gregorian chants are still circumspect in regard to listening to the melodious incantations of *vos zugt Rava, vos zugt Abaye* that emanate from the halls of any yeshiva. So the Torah tells us to eschew the actions of Egyptians no matter how politically correct they may be. For there are no better *chukim* to try to understand — and to follow — than those that come from your very own home.

PARSHAS KEDOSHIM

➣ *Burden of Reproof*

$\mathcal{I}$n this *parsha*, the Torah not only teaches the basics of getting along with one's neighbor, it also codifies the elementary rules of behavior that set a moral standard for social interaction. "You shall not be a gossipmonger . . . you shall not stand idly by while your brother's blood is shed . . . you shall not hate your brother in your heart . . . you shall not take revenge" (*Leviticus* 19:16-18). In one matter, however, the Torah also exhorts the Jewish people to act in a way that many might believe would cause neighbors to distance themselves: the Torah says to reprove a fellow-Jew.

Obviously, the concept of "live and let live" is foreign to Judaism. In fact, the *mitzvah* of reproof is placed immediately following the verse, "you shall not stand idly by while your brother's blood is shed."

Indeed, in the Torah's view spiritual distress is equivalent to physical distress. Just as a Jew cannot stand idly by when someone is drowning physically, so, too, a Jew must act when someone is drowning spiritually. But the Torah does more than merely tell the Jewish people to admonish — it tells us how to do it.

"You shall not hate your brother in your heart; reprove, you shall surely reprove your fellow, and do not bear a sin upon him." The last part of the charge is difficult to understand. What does the Torah mean, "and do not bear a sin upon him?"

Rashi explains that the Torah does not want a Jew to sin while reproving a fellow Jew — "do not embarrass him publicly."

The actual text, however, seems to read to "not bear a sin upon him," the sinner. How can we understand this?

As the Chofetz Chaim traveled through Poland, Lithuania, and Russia to sell his works, he entered an inn in Vilna and beheld a disturbing sight. A burly young man was about to devour a roasted and stuffed hen that lay on his plate. A tall stein, overflowing with cold brew, stood next to the succulent fowl. All of a sudden, the man picked up the entire hen and stuffed it into his mouth. Washing down his meal with a giant gulp of beer, he left the stein nearly empty. The Chofetz Chaim had never seen a Jewish person eat like that, let alone without a *bracha* (blessing)!

The Sage turned to the innkeeper and inquired, "Tell me a little about this man. I'd like to talk to him."

"Oh!" the host smirked while waving his hand in disgust. "There's nobody to talk to. This young man never learned a day in his life. The Cantonists captured him when he was 11, and he served in the Russian army for 15 years. He hardly observes any *mitzvos*. It's truly amazing that he is concerned with eating kosher!" Then the innkeeper smiled. "But I'm sure I can count on him for a three-course meal every Thursday night!"

The Chofetz Chaim was neither shocked nor amused. He simply walked over to the former soldier and shook his greasy hand warmly. After a sincere greeting, the Chofetz Chaim introduced himself and spoke. "I heard that you actually survived the cruel Russian army of Czar Nicholas. I am sure that many times the terrible officers tried to convert you or at least force you to eat non-kosher. Yet you remained a steadfast Jew!"

Tears welled in the Chofetz Chaim's eyes as he continued talking. "I only wish that I would be guaranteed a place in the World-To-Come as you will be. What strength! What fortitude! You have withstood harsher tests than the sages of old."

The soldier looked up from his plate, and tears welled in his eyes, too. He leaned over and kissed the hand of the elderly Sage.

Then the Chofetz Chaim continued. "I am sure that if you get yourself a teacher and continue your life as a true Torah-observant Jew, there will be no one in this world who is as fortunate as you!"

According to Rabbi M. M. Yasher, the biographer of the Chofetz Chaim, the soldier became a pupil of the Chofetz Chaim and eventually became a great *tzadik* (righteous Jew).

⭢≫⭠

Perhaps with the words, "do not bear a sin upon him", the verse is stating a greater message: We should not focus on the action of a sin alone when admonishing someone. The Torah wants each Jew to find a positive aspect in another person that will help raise his holy soul from its murky depths.

It is easy to enumerate a friend's misdeeds — and perhaps even easier to tell him off. But that is not the goal.

Mishlei tells us, "He who acclaims evildoers as righteous will be cursed. But those who admonish will be blessed" (*Proverbs* 24:24-25). Rabbi Shlomo Alkabetz of Tzfat explained that the two verses work in tandem. They teach that although false flattery is abhorrent, when it is used to admonish by finding the good in those who have strayed, it is to be commended. The Torah wants the Jewish people to elevate a person, instead of thrusting the burden of his sins upon him. In that manner, a Jew won't bully his fellow; instead, he will build him up. Finding faults in others, bears a great responsibility. Not only do the Jewish people bear the difficult and sensitive burden of proof, we bear an equally difficult and sensitive burden of reproof.

PARSHAS EMOR

➣ Mantel Bread

*T*owards the end of *Parshas Emor*, the Torah details the *mitzvah* of the *Lechem Hapanim* (Temple showbreads). These breads were baked weekly and placed on the gold table in the Holy Temple (*Leviticus* 24:5-9). Immediately following these laws, the Torah relates the story of the blasphemer. "And the son of an Israelite woman, whose father was Egyptian, went out among the Children of Israel . . . and cursed Hashem" (*Leviticus* 24:10-11).

Though the Torah does not mention the content of the man's evil words, there are various *Midrashic* accounts. Rabbi Berachia, noting the juxtaposition of the story, explains that the law is that once a week, each Friday, the *Lechem Hapanim* were baked and placed on the golden table for *Shabbos*. They sat for a week, then fresh bread was displayed while the old bread was given to the *kohanim* (priests). Miraculously, however, the bread remained fresh for the entire week, a fact which irked the blasphemer. "What kind of ritual is this?" he cried. "Shall the 'King of kings' be honored with week-old bread? The Supreme Deity deserves no less than fresh bread daily!" The man then went on to mock a system he did not comprehend and ultimately blasphemed the Master Recipient of the observance — Hashem. For many years I was never able to understand the psyche of this Jew. He began by legitimately questioning a difficult observance. After all, if we are assumedly giving Hashem anthropomorphic qualities by offering Him bread, why should we not offer Him fresh bread daily? With this question, it seems that the man demonstrated a true adoration for Hashem and wanted the best for his Master. Feeling that old bread was an abomination, he did not want to see his Master sustain its freshness through supernatural intervention. So how did these feelings result in his cursing the very God he cared so much for?

＊＊＊

> Once, an elderly woman approached my father in shul with a beautiful *mantel* (Torah cover) she had made from rich blue velvet. My father took the Torah scroll out of the Ark and immediately placed the new *mantel* over it. He was about to exclaim how lovely it was when both the woman and my father realized the *mantel* was at least six inches shorter than the Torah scroll. "Rabbi," the woman proclaimed, "that's no problem. My handiwork is so beautiful. Couldn't you just trim the lower half of the Torah to fit it?" He smiled and said, "I'm sorry, but the Torah doesn't get modified. I guess you'll just have to lengthen your *mantel*."

＊＊＊

All people have personal visions of moral edification. We philosophize, rationalize, and moralize — all in attempt to reconcile comfortably the ramifications of our actions with our conscience. If what the Torah instructs us does not fit into our pre-conceived vision of God's will, we often change the Torah's dictates or create new interpretations rather than inconvenience ourselves or change our perceptions.

The definition of what is right is often derived from what a person wants or perceives. An unshakable premise is then formulated — and everything in its way is blasphemed and mutilated. As such, people may establish moral imperatives from certain Torah readings and then create new interpretations that may in fact deride Torah values. One must remember that each word is from Hashem, albeit often difficult to comprehend. Thus, our job is to follow the Torah in its entirety, not to grandstand on certain issues or use moral derivations to deride the Torah's more difficult commands. We can't decide that God needs fresh loaves of bread and then deride the God Who asks for week-old bread!

Our creativity must not define the Torah — it must instead be defined by Torah. If our ideas clash with the written word of Hashem, they are ipso facto expressions of our personal desires.

We must recognize them as such and leave them on the side, for we have a strong and vital constitution that tells us how to honor our most cherished value: the Torah.

PARSHAS BEHAR

✍ *Home Free All*

*I*t is probably the most famous Biblical verse in American history. Each year, many thousands of people come to see its bold, raised lettering prominently encircling the rim of the most revered icon of our country's independence. Yet many visitors hardly notice the words.

Instead, their gaze is transfixed upon another, much less divine symbol, one that bears the painful message of that sacred verse. But the large crack they come to see has no inherent meaning; it is only the result of the constant sounding of the words that are enshrined on its oxidized metal, words from this portion, "Proclaim liberty throughout the land and to all its inhabitants thereof" (*Leviticus* 25:10).

Truth be told, however, those words refer not to a revolution or a liberation: the phrase refers instead to the *mitzvah* of *Yovel* — jubilee. Every 50 years, all Jewish servants, whether employed for only a six-year period or a longer period, including those who truly desire to remain as servants to their masters, are freed. They return home to their families; their career of indenture is over.

Yet the verse is confusing. "Proclaim liberty throughout the land and to all its inhabitants thereof:" isn't the Torah referring to the freedom of slaves and the servants? Isn't this a proclamation of freedom for a select few? Why would the Torah use the words "and to all its inhabitants" when only some of its inhabitants are going free? The masters and employers were never slaves; they are not going free. Or are they?

In the first volume of his prolific *Maggid* series, Rabbi Paysach Krohn relates the following story:

It was a cold and blustery afternoon, and Rabbi Isser Zalman Melzer, the dean of the Eitz Chaim Yeshiva in Jerusalem, was returning home from a long day in the yeshiva. Accompanied by his nephew, Reb Dovid Finkel, who normally walked him home, Rabbi Melzer began to ascend the steps to his Jerusalem apartment. Suddenly, Rabbi Melzer stopped and retreated down the old staircase as if he had forgotten something. When he reached the street, he began to wander aimlessly back and forth, deep in thought. Concerned, his nephew began to question the strange actions of the great Torah sage. "Did Reb Isser Zalman forget something?" the younger man asked. "Why doesn't he enter his home?"

The wind began to blow even harder, but despite the chill Reb Isser Zalman remained outside his home. After 15 minutes had passed, once again Rabbi Melzer walked slowly up the stairs, waited, and then headed back down.

His nephew could not contain himself. "Please, Rebbe," he pleaded. "What's the matter?" Reb Isser Zalman just shrugged and said, "Just wait a few more moments. Please."

"But Uncle," the young man protested, "it's getting cold. Please answer me. What are you waiting for?"

Rabbi Melzer realized that he could no longer keep his motivations to himself. "I'll explain," he said. "As I walked up the steps I heard the young woman who comes once a week to help with the housework. She was mopping the kitchen floor and singing while she worked. I knew that if I were to walk in she would become embarrassed and stop her singing. Since singing helps her through her work, I did not want to make her task any harder, let alone deny her the joy of her songs. So, despite the cold, I decided to wait outside until she finishes her work and her song. Then I'll go in."

※

The Torah uses a very significant expression that synopsizes the true meaning of ownership and servitude. "Proclaim liberty throughout the land and to all its inhabitants thereof." When one employs someone, he is also indebted to his employee. In addition to giving a paycheck, an employer is responsible for the worker's feelings, working conditions, and general welfare. He is obligated to provide a safe environment, suitable provisions, and, above all, behave with *mentchlichkeit* (decency). So when *Yovel* arrives, and the workers and servants return home, they are not the only ones who go free. A great burden is lifted from the shoulders of the masters as well. Freedom is declared for *all* the inhabitants of the land. So, the servants are not the only ones who are home free. As we used to say in the heat of a game of ring-o-le-vio, we are "home free — all."

PARSHAS B'CHUKOSAI

✒ Out of the Depths

This portion contains the *Tochacha*, the stern admonitions and harsh warnings concerning what will happen to the Jewish people should they not observe the Torah. Of course, the predictions of misfortune are preceded by a bounty of blessings — dependent on whether or not the Jewish people keep the Torah. Unfortunately, however, the bad comes with the good, and the penalties are not omitted. Indeed, they are hauntingly clear and undiluted.

The Torah details calamity upon calamity with unerring Divine accuracy. Predicting that enemies speaking foreign tongues will come from foreign lands to capture the Jewish nation, the Torah forewarns that these conquerors will not act like most — leaving the subjugated in their own land. Instead, the conquerors will disperse the Jews throughout the entire world. In frightful detail, the *parsha* foreshadows the horrors of the Inquisition, the Holocaust, and more, with descriptions of barbarism, Jews betraying Jews, and mass starvation. Indeed, the predictions are amazing in their accuracy and equally depressing — the Jewish nation was the victim.

It's a very difficult *parsha*, but the Torah *must* apprise the Jewish people of the pain and suffering we would eventually endure.

Yet the Torah doesn't end its *Tochacha* on a note of despair. The strong admonitions close with a promise that, although the Jewish people will be spread throughout the world, we will always yearn for our homeland, feel connected to it, and have an enduring love for Judaism and our Father in Heaven that will never cease. Thousands of years and countless massacres, crusades, pogroms, and inquisitions later, that love still perseveres. Pretty powerful.

Indeed that promise would have been a great way to end a depressing portion — as well as *Sefer Vayikra*. But the Torah ends the portion — and the book — with an anticlimactic group of laws.

Immediately after the *Tochacha*, the Torah discusses the laws of *erechin*: a person has the right to donate his own value, or the value of any of his possessions, to the Holy Temple. Suprisingly, the Torah does indeed assess a value to any living soul, and that value, whether 30 shekels or 50 shekels, is to be donated to the Holy Temple.

My question is what connection does this last part of the *parsha* have to the stern and ominous sections which precede it?

~~~

After the Nazis invaded the small village of Klausenberg, they began to celebrate in their usual sadistic fashion. Gathering the Jews into a circle in the center of town, the Nazis then paraded the Rebbe, Rabbi Yekusial Yehuda Halberstam, into the middle. Taunting and teasing him, pulling his beard and pushing him around, the vile soldiers trained their guns on Rabbi Halberstam as the commander began to speak. "Tell us, Rabbi," the officer sneered, "do you really believe that you are the Chosen People?"

The soldiers guarding the crowd howled in laughter. But the Rebbe did not. In a serene voice, he answered loudly and clearly, "Most certainly."

The officer became enraged, lifted his rifle above his head and severely beat the Rebbe. As the Rebbe fell to the ground, there was rage in the officer's voice. "Do you still think you are the Chosen People?" he yelled.

Once again, the Rebbe nodded his head and said, "Yes, we are."

The officer became even more infuriated, kicked the Rebbe in the shin and repeated, "You stupid Jew, you lie here on the ground, beaten and humiliated. What makes you think that you are part of the Chosen People?"

From the depths of his humiliation and clouded in dust, the Rebbe replied, "As long as we are not the ones kicking and beating innocent people, we can call ourselves Chosen."

———✦———

The Kotzker Rebbe explains that the Torah follows the *Tochacha*, the story of Jews kicked and beaten from their homeland, with an even more powerful message. No matter what happens, we have enormous value as individuals and as a nation, now and for eternity. Hashem understands that even in the depths of the Diaspora each and every one of us is a great commodity.

Even lying on the ground, beaten and degraded, a Jewish man, woman, or child can declare his value to the Holy Temple. For no matter how low any nation considers him, God values his enormous worth — he is considered cherished for eternity, until the great day when all the nations of the world will also realize the precious value of the tiny nation that dwells among them.

ספר במדבר

The Book of

Numbers

PARSHAS BAMIDBAR

☞ Counted Out

*T*he Book of Numbers begins just that way — with many numbers. It counts the Jews who were in the desert and then assigns unique flags and positions for each of the tribes in the great camp of Israel. Strategically situated around the *Mishkan*, the tribes are grouped according to status and rank. Yet, this division is somewhat troubling. Why isn't there a great melting pot under one flag?

Moreover, singling out the tribe of *Levi* raises more questions. "Bring the tribe of *Levi* close and have them stand before Ahron, the *Kohen*, and they shall serve him" *(Numbers* 3:6). The Torah also relates the specific tasks of the descendants of *Levi* and warns the stranger, the ordinary Israelite, against attempting to join in performing those tasks. Why is there even further division in the ranks of Jews? Why can't the Israelite do the task of the *Kohen*, and the *Kohen* the task of the *Levi*, and the *Levi* the task of the Israelite?

※

In the late 1930s, the great Arturo Toscanini was conducting the New York Philharmonic Orchestra performing Beethoven's Leonore No. 3 Overture. This particular outdoor concert was held at City College's Lewiston Stadium and was exceptionally well attended. The famed trumpeter Harry Glanz was going to play offstage trumpet solo, an integral part of the production of this symphonic masterpiece.

Indeed, people had flocked to hear the great trumpeter perform under the baton of the legendary Toscanini. When the time came, Glanz positioned himself in a corner about 50 feet behind the stage ready to play his notes. As the concert led up to the key moment, Toscanini held his baton high, pausing to hear the sharp blasts of Glanz's horn. They never came. All Toscannini saw was a burly security guard wrestling with the hapless musician on the grass behind the stage.

The guard was pointing to the stage. "You fool!" he was shouting, "what do you think you're doing blowing that horn back here? Don't you see there's a concert going on up there?"

━━━

Not everybody who desires to can be up on the stage. In the concert of the Almighty, every player has his designated position and helps to make the symphony beautiful. I have a friend who travels throughout the United States and attends *minyanim* all across the country. "Often," he says, "when they ask, 'is there a *Kohen* in the house?' I have the urge to go up there and pretend that I am a *Kohen*, because I always wanted to know what it's like being called up first!"

Fortunately, he, like most of us, understands that every person in the nation of Israel, whether man or woman, has a unique role to play. Sometimes these roles are played from the inside, sometimes from the outside; nevertheless, the offstage trumpeters are just as vital as the onstage ones. And if we rush the stage to perform out of sync, we can ruin the beautiful harmony of a carefully orchestrated experience.

The Israelite has specific *mitzvos* that the *kohen* cannot perform. He may visit the dying and assist in the burial of any deceased. It is the Israelite who gives tithes and supports the poor. The *kohen* and *levi* inherit no land, which gives rise to myriad commandments. True, the Israelite cannot serve in the Temple, but his trumpeting may resound as loud as his brother's. As long as he plays it in the right position.

PARSHAS NASO

➣ *Small Talk*

*T*his *parsha* contains a number of exciting episodes. It details the Halachos of the suspected adulterous woman, her fate and that of her convicted illicit partner. The *parsha* also delineates the rules and regulations of the *nazir,* one who abstains from certain worldly pleasures by eschewing wine and leaving his hair uncut.

Yet, tucked away in the midst of these difficult episodes are the priestly blessings — five verses that shine an encouraging light in the midst of a complex portion. "May *Hashem* bless you and keep you. May *Hashem* shine His countenance on you and be gracious to you. May *Hashem* lift His countenance upon you and establish you in peace" *(Numbers* 6:24-26).

Less celebrated, however, are the verses that appear immediately *before* and *after* the actual blessings. "Thus shall you bless the Children of Israel; speak to them" *(Numbers* 6:23). What is the importance — and the meaning — of the extra words, "speak to them?" *Hashem* charges the priests with the actual verses of blessing, and He ends with an additional command: "Place My Name upon the Children of Israel, and I shall bless them" *(Numbers* 6:27). Again, the verse leaves us wondering — of course, it is *Hashem* Who will bless them, but what does His Name have to do with it? Didn't He just prescribe the formula? Why aren't the three verses enough to spur God's blessings?

━━━

A short time after my family came to Woodmere, a lovely young Israeli couple with two young children moved next door to us. After conversing with them, my wife and I realized that they were not in the least

bit observant of Jewish tradition. They had never observed Yom Kippur, let alone *Shabbos* or *kashrus*. It seemed to us that the reason they moved to America was because Israel was becoming too religious for them.

While my wife and I felt a strong responsibility to bring these fine people closer to *Torah,* we did not feel comfortable telling them about laws that they must have known something about but chose not to observe.

Fortunately, Rabbi Shlomo Freifeld, the great *Rosh Yeshiva* who brought thousands of people close to Torah, lived in our neighborhood. I explained our situation to him and asked, "Rebbe, what do you do to make someone *frum* (religious)?"

He smiled and put his large hand on my shoulder. "Do absolutely nothing," he said. I stood shocked and confused as he continued.

"Be a *mentsh,*" he said. "Never miss a 'good morning' or a 'good afternoon.' Make sure your lawn is neat and your children well behaved. And just be friendly." Then Rabbi Freifeld quoted words from our sages, "Make sure that the name of *Hashem* is cherished through you." He paused, looked me in the eye, and proclaimed confidently, "Follow that advice and you will not have to do a thing. Through you they will come closer to the *Torah.*"

We followed his advice. We invited the couple to our home for meals, and our children played together. I talked politics with him, while my wife discussed gardening with her. We spoke about everything — except religion. I was therefore shocked when, in October, our neighbors asked us where the closest synagogue was: they had decided to go to *shul* for Yom Kippur. I was even more surprised when days later they asked for my help in building a *sukkah.*

I am sad to relate that eventually we lost our very good neighbors. After five years of living in the United States, they decided to move back to Israel. America was becoming too gentile for them!

Before it cites the actual blessings, the *Torah* teaches us the true way to bless Jews — "speak to them." Indeed, the words "speak to them" may be more important than the actual blessing. The famed Chofetz Chaim charged my wife's grandfather, Rabbi Laizer Levin, Rabbi of Detroit for 50 years, with a simple message: *"Reb Laizer, gei rehd tzu Yidden"* (Reb Laizer, go speak to Jews).

The priestly blessings do not end much differently. "Place My Name upon the Children of Israel, and I shall bless them." When *Hashem's* Name is placed upon His nation, then blessing is sure to follow.

A smile, a hello, a good *Shabbos* or *Shabbat Shalom*, may be the key to forging a different attitude in an otherwise skeptical Jew. To paraphrase an astronaut who reached higher physical spheres, "One small word to man can produce giants for mankind."

The true blessing does not come from theological incantations; it comes instead from the simple and sincere words from the lips and smiles of the heart.

PARSHAS B'HALOS'CHA

➢ *Manna & Power*

*I*t seems that some people cannot appreciate something special! Imagine: the Jews were treated to the heavenly gift of manna, yet they complained about it.

The manna was a supernatural delicacy that fell from the heavens and sustained the Jewish nation during its 40-year sojourn in the desert. Indeed, the heavenly food had the ability to transform itself to please the palate of even the most advanced culinary critic, tasting exactly the way its eater desired it to taste! Whether Belgian waffles with ice cream, or steak with hash browns, through mere thought the eater was able to transform the manna's flavor into something most delicious.

Yet the Jewish nation was still not happy. "We remember the free fish that we ate in Egypt" (*Numbers* 11:5) they exclaimed. The *Talmud* questions the words "free fish." "Since when," the *Talmud* asks, "was anything free in the land of slavery?" The *Talmud* answers that the word "free" means free from *mitzvos* (commandments). Because they had not yet received their charge at Sinai, the Jews had no *mitzvos* to observe during their exile in Egypt. Therefore, they recalled the free fish that they ate during the Egyptian bondage. The obvious question is, what does food — fish or manna — have to do with freedom? Why did the Jews complain about their new responsibilities and intrinsically link them with the miraculous bread? If so, was it the miraculous bread that changed their status? And why did they link fish with freedom?

〜〜〜

Rabbi Dr. Abraham Twerski tells a wonderful story that took place in Europe.

Little Chaim sat in the back row of his *cheder*. One day, the rebbe, a stern fellow who had little patience with his young charges, called Chaim to recite the letters of the *Aleph-Bet*. The teacher took a long stick and pointed to the letter *Aleph*. "*Vos iz das?* (What is this?)" he shouted.

Chaim looked him straight in the eye, shrugged his shoulders, and said nothing.

Whack! The stick came down solidly on the boy's hand. "I said, '*Vos iz das!*'" the teacher screamed, tapping his stick fiercely on the letter.

Again, Chaim jutted out his lower lip and shrugged his shoulders even higher. He spread out his hands, palms up, offering a sacrifice to the altar of the dreaded stick, while intoning, "I have no idea what that letter is!"

His offering duly accepted, once again the frustrated teacher brought the stick down on poor Chaim's hand. After futile attempts to have Chaim pronounce the *Aleph*, the teacher went to the next student, who proceeded to recite the entire *Aleph-Bet* flawlessly.

After class, Chaim's friends surrounded him. "We don't understand," they stated in uniform amazement. "Everybody knows the letter *Aleph*! When the rebbe pointed to the *Aleph*, why didn't you just tell him 'It's an *Aleph*'?"

Chaim smiled. "I'm smarter than that," he said. "Of course, I knew what the letter was! But I also knew that the moment I said '*Aleph*,' our rebbe would point to the *Bet* and ask me what that is. Then he'd point to the *Gimmel* and *Daled*. Soon, I'd have to recite the entire *Aleph-Bet*! So I'd rather take a few whacks at the beginning and not have to go through the whole ordeal!"

The commentaries explain that when the Jewish people reminisced about free fish they remembered an era when they had no spiritual or moral responsibilities. The Jews understood that when one eats manna — the fare of the angels — angelic responsibility accompanies the gastronomic action. The Jews would have rather foregone the miraculous manna in order to be freed of the obligations it brought. They did not want to recite even the *Aleph* in the knowledge that an obligation to recite the *Bet* and *Gimmel* would naturally follow.

Often in life, we hesitate to take the first step. Though that particular step may be simple and uncomplicated, we fear to begin treading because we are fully aware of where those first steps may lead us. Accepting responsibility is, however, the role of a people to whom the world looks for moral and spiritual guidance.

As such, the first bite of a new undertaking will surely be deliciously challenging, while the second bite will perhaps be a little more difficult to swallow. Nevertheless, when taken this way, at the end of the meal no one will have bitten off more than he can swallow.

Those who have dined on the fare of leadership will come to realize that the food of accomplishment is as delicious as anyone's wildest imagination. It may even be spiritually delicious — perhaps as delicious as the manna itself.

PARSHAS SHELACH

✒ *Chicken Yiddle*

"The sky is falling!" they shouted. Well not quite, but when the ten spies who went to examine the Land of Israel brought back tales of armed cities and mighty and formidable enemies they threw a confident nation into sheer terror. It is almost inconceivable that a nation which saw a sea split and Egypt humbled would cringe in utter terror — because of reports of giants and fortified cities in their new country.

The *Midrash* details the episode: upon returning to the Jewish camp, the ten spies dispersed amongst their own families and began to bemoan their fate. "Woe is to us!" they cried. "Our daughters will be taken captive, our sons murdered, and our possessions looted!"

Neighbor to neighbor, the tales spread, and within hours the entire nation was in a rebellious uproar, ignoring the positive reports that Calev and Yehoshua brought back. The Jewish people even besieged Moshe, demanding to return to Egypt.

The Torah details the Jews' hysterical reaction to the malicious tales of gloom. Yet, it seems that it was not the tales of fortified cities or the sight of mutated-looking giant fruits or even the actual giants themselves that caused the Jews to lament. The way the story is related, the actual wailing and rebellion occurred only after they heard an interesting detail. The spies described the giant men whom they encountered and the way they felt during that experience. "And there we saw the sons of giants; we felt in our own eyes like grasshoppers next to them" (*Numbers* 13:33). Immediately, the next verse tells us, "The entire assembly raised up their voices and wept that night . . . saying if only we had died in the land of Egypt or . . . in the wilderness!" *(Numbers* 14:1-3). It seems that the final words of the spies, "we felt in our *own* eyes like grasshoppers," set up this tragic and futile reaction. Why?

My brother, Rabbi Zvi Kamenetzky, loves telling the following story:

Yankel, one of Warsaw's poorer folk, received a first-class train ticket from a wealthy cousin to visit him in Lodz. Yankel arrived at the station clutching his ticket tightly. He had never taken a train before and had no idea where to go. He spotted some well-dressed individuals and just knew he was not sitting with them. Then in the far corner of the waiting room he noticed a group of vagrants with packs on their shoulders, their eyes shifting back and forth. Yankel meandered toward them, figuring that their place was his. The first-class passengers began to board, but the vagrants still waited. All of a sudden, the whistle blew and the train began to move. The vagabonds quickly jumped aboard the baggage car, Yankel following in pursuit. He slithered into the dark car and lay with them underneath a pile of suitcases, still clutching his ticket in fear.

He endured the bumps and heat of the baggage car and figured that such was his fate until the door of the baggage compartment flew open and a burly conductor flanked by two policemen entered. They began moving baggage and bags until they spotted poor Yankel and his friends cowering in a corner. The large conductor loomed over them and asked with a sneer in his voice, "Can I see your tickets?"

Yankel, hiding in a corner, looked up from under his coat to see the officers staring at him. He emerged from the group, shaking, and presented the sweat-infused ticket that he had been clutching ever-so-tightly during the entire ordeal.

The conductor looked at it carefully and then began to laugh hysterically. "Young man," he barked, "you have a first-class ticket! What are you doing here lying with these dregs in the baggage compartment? When you have a first-class ticket, you ought to act like a first-class passenger!"

The Jewish nation had no fear of giant fruit or giant men. They knew they had leaders who could overcome any obstacle. After all, Moshe had led them across the Red Sea. Yehoshua and Chur had helped defeat Amalck. But when they heard the ten spies — princes of the tribes — claim that they felt like insects, they knew that they had no chance to conquer the land of Israel. They had nothing left to do but cry. Because if you are holding a first-class ticket but act as if you are an itinerant, then your ticket is worthless.

The giant fruit, fortified cities, and powerful giants — all tiny acorns compared to the power of the Almighty — suddenly loomed large. And the sky began to fall on a self-pitying nation that was led by self-pitying leaders. And with the falling sky fell the dreams, hopes, and aspirations of a generation that once yearned to dwell in the land of their forefathers. The Jewish nation was left to ponder that message for 40 years in the desert — and perhaps thousands of years in the Diaspora.

That is what happens when mighty princes with first-class tickets to paradise think that they are tiny grasshoppers holding tickets to nowhere.

PARSHAS KORACH

➤ Blind Ambition

*L*ove is blind. So is hate and any principle that begins to shade the intellect with emotion. In this *parsha*, in what appears to be the worst ideological division of the Jewish people after the Exodus, a litmus test of human nature proved that the great divide bordered more on ego than on principle.

Korach, a cousin of Moshe and a brilliant man in his own right, began a rebellion that challenged the leadership and divine appointment of both Moshe and Ahron. In addition to his own family, Korach's iconoclastic actions inspired 250 Jewish leaders to denounce publicly the leadership of Moshe and Ahron. Foremost among the self-appointed detractors were two men with a history of vindictive activities toward Moshe — Dassan and Aviram. Back in Egypt, when Moshe killed an Egyptian taskmaster who was beating an innocent Jew, these men threatened to inform the Egyptian authorities.

But Moshe wanted to deal with them. As leader of two million people, he could have laughed at the complaints of a minute fraction of the population, but he didn't. He reached out to Dassan and Aviram and asked them to come and discuss their qualms with him. His request was met with a barrage of insults.

"Even if you gouge out our eyes, we shall not go up!" they responded (*Cf. Numbers* 16:14).

I was always amazed at this most arrogant response. Why did these men, who obviously were stubborn, arrogant, and supercilious, respond in a self-deprecating manner? Why did they suggest the horrific infliction of eye-gouging upon themselves? Would it not be enough to respond, even to one's worst enemy, "We will not come"? What connection does the loss of vision have with their refusal?

Reb Gimpel, a travelling salesman, developed an illness in a small village far from his home and was prescribed with a cure that entailed eating non-kosher food. Since he was a foreigner in that town, he decided to ask the local rabbi if he was permitted to take the medicine.

The gentile doctor did not know where the rabbi lived and suggested that Reb Gimpel ask the local butcher. Reb Gimpel went into the butcher shop. "Excuse me," he asked the burly meat vendor, "do you know where I can find your rabbi?" "The rabbi!" sneered the butcher, "why would a respectable-looking man like yourself need our rabbi?" The man was puzzled but continued to explain. "I'd like to ask him something."

"Ask him something!" mocked the butcher. "Our rabbi doesn't know the difference between a horse and a cow! You're wasting your time! Ask the *chazzan* where he lives; I have no reason to tell you."

The shocked man went to the *chazzan's* home. "Excuse me," he asked, "do you know where the rabbi lives?"

"The rabbi?" asked the cantor in horror. "Why in the world would you want to meet that ignoramus? Surely you don't want to ask him a question! I wouldn't want to be party to your misfortune. Better ask the *mohel.*"

Frustrated, the poor man went to the home of the *mohel,* where once again he was shocked by the barrage of insults and put-downs directed toward the rabbi. Finally, however, the *mohel* acquiesced and directed the man to the rabbi's home. The man entered the threshold and before he even shook the rabbi's hand he exclaimed, "Listen, I don't know you, and you don't know me. I came here to ask one question, but I will ask you something totally different. Why are you the rabbi here? The butcher thinks you're a fool, the *chazzan* thinks you're an ignoramus, and the *mohel* loathes you. Why in the world do you remain the rabbi of this town?"

The rabbi looked up from his bifocals and smiled. "Ah! The insults, the abuse, and the criticism. But you know what: for a little honor it's all worth it!"

———

As the proverbial rabble-rousers of all time, Dassan and Aviram were shedding profound insight into the laws of arrogance. When one is set on a self-fulfilling mission of squabbling, as corrupt and perverted as his judgment may be, so is his vision. He is blind to the critics, blind to the world, and worst of all, blind to his own self. Once a man is blind, you can gouge out his eyes and he will not notice.

Only those with a pure sense of mission possess the vision to see a situation from every aspect — even if it differs from their own. Moshe asked to meet his worst enemies and try to see their point of view. His myopic enemies, however, would rather be blinded. But I guess for a little bit of principle, it's worth it.

Parshas Chukas

⟿ *Mystery and History*

*T*he laws of the *parah adumah*, the red heifer, have enraptured mortals since the day it was commanded. Because there was no reason or rationale given for this *mitzvah*, the nations of the world, baffled by it, have mocked our observance of it. Even King Solomon, the wisest of men, claimed to be confused by its reasoning. Indeed, Moshe was the only mortal who ever understood its every nuance.

The laws *are* complex, symbolism mysterious, and their logic quite enigmatic. The red heifer's ashes purify those who have become *tamei* (ritually impure), yet the administrating *kohen* who was *tahor* (pure) becomes *tamei*. There is no underlying logic or reason for those occurrences; yet that is the law — clearly stated in this week's portion. So sacred was the offering of the particular red heifer that Moshe and Ahron prepared, that its ashes were saved from generation to generation. The ashes of each additional red heifer offering were added to the remnants of the previous one, so that the new ashes mixed with the vestigial ashes of Moshe's original red heifer. As such, the ensuing generations and the thousands of *kohanim* and Israelites who performed the *mitzvah* of *parah adumah* believed with unquestioning faith in the law's ritual Divinity and spiritual power.

Why were these complex, very spiritual laws placed in the middle of the book of *Bamidbar*? The enigmatic laws of ritual purity and impurity are almost entirely relegated to *Sefer Vayikra* (*Leviticus*). Indeed, that *sefer* discusses sacrificial offerings, also detailing a host of physio-spiritual states, among them *tzora'as*, *zav*, *zavah*, *nidah*, and so on. Shouldn't the mystical requirements of the *parah adumah* join its counterparts along with the laws of *kohanim*? Why, instead, is it placed in the book that recounts the stories of human folly — the malicious uprising of *Korach*, the miscalculations of the spies, the unfaithfulness of the *sotah*, the complaints against the heavenly fare of manna? What significance does the juxtaposition of this seemingly unexplainable divine ritual, obviously not congruent with mortal logic, have for the tales of human error and miscalculation?

One evening during World War II, Senator Kenneth McKellar of Tennessee could not sleep. As chairman of the Senate Appropriations Committee, he could not understand why he should approve the administration's request of some $2 billion towards certain unusual scientific research.

He called Secretary of War Henry L. Stimson and began to shout, "Do you expect me to sanction this enormous appropriation without any idea as to where it is going?"

Stimson kept quiet, pondering and hesitating, then finally asked, "Can you keep a secret?" After McKellar assured him that he could, Stimson whispered, "We are about to split the atom."

McKellar exploded. "Are you crazy? This is a war! We have men out there! We need guns! We need planes! We need ammunition! And you guys are fooling around with some hocus pocus — splitting atoms!"

It was only months later that McKellar, along with the entire world, learned the power of this seemingly incomprehensible and esoteric exercise.

Perhaps there is no better place to expound the laws of *parah adumah* than in the middle of *Sefer Bamidbar*. For it is this *Torah* section that also discusses a generation that thought they were able to calculate and define everything. This Book tells of spies who returned from Canaan and exclaimed that according to their calculations there was no logical way that Israel could conquer the land. The *Book of Numbers* tells of Korach, who complained that according to his calculations he should have been prince of the tribe of *Levi*. The *Midrash* tells of Korach gathering 250 men and ranting that according to his logic a *mezuzah* is unnecessary in a room filled with sacred books. *Bamidbar* talks about false leaders who would be satisfied if only the spirit of the law is fulfilled, but not the letter. It even contains the story of Miriam, who, according to her reasoning, rationalized speaking ill of her brother Moshe. It discusses Jews who wanted meat rather than manna.

So actually there is no better time and place to talk about the red heifer and its complex and esoteric laws than the *sefer* in which humans make incorrect mortal calculations to redefine *Torah* outlook and Divine direction.

The red cow and its laws represent the complete omnipotence of *Hashem*, be it in spirit, in logic, or in mechanics. The laws of the red heifer exclaim that though we may search for rhyme and reason in *Torah*, we still must observe the *mitzvos* it commands, regardless if we understand them or not. For there will *always* be some aspect that may appear to us as mysterious as hocus pocus. Yet with uncalculating faith we must understand that there is great Divine method to the many aspects we cannot fathom. In that manner we shall merit to be committed totally to *Hashem's Torah*, and not to our mortal vision of it.

PARSHAS BALAK

*Y*ou have to approach something from the right angle. At least that's what Balak the King of Moab tried to convince his prime sorcerer who was futilely trying to curse the Jewish nation. Though Bilaam had a notorious reputation for curses that never failed and an ability to cast spells upon whomever he desired, his powers didn't work against the Jews. He tried, at a great price, to curse the Jewish nation camped opposite Moab; but each time Bilaam opened his mouth, blessings and not curses were emitted. "How beautiful are your tents, Jacob," Bilaam said. "How can I curse when God is not angry?"

Each time the mission failed, King Balak flew into a rage. Bilaam tried to subvert God's intentions and appease Him with sacrifices — all to no avail.

Balak tried another strategy, saying, "Come with me to a different place; from there you will see them; however, you will see [the camp's] edge and not all of it — and you will curse it for me from there" *(Numbers 23:13)*. This idea didn't work either.

Yet this new strategy is confusing. What's the difference if Bilaam were to see *all* of Israel, or if he would stand in a place that offers only a *partial* view? Is the God of Israel not ever-present, protecting them in part as well as in whole? Why would a curse take effect when Israel's detractors view only a fraction of Israel?

Many a ballad singer and storyteller have recounted the story of Yossele the Holy Miser of Crakow. Yossele, the story goes, was lying on his deathbed. The *Chevra Kadisha* (burial society) who

gathered around him threatened that unless he made a substantial contribution to the poor before his death, they would refuse to bury him. Yossele refused and shortly thereafter passed away.

True to their word the *Chevra,* along with the townsfolk, refused to get involved with a man whom people said gave no charity whatsoever. Yossele's body lay for days until the Rabbi commanded the townsfolk to bury him. They did — in a pauper's grave on the outskirts of the cemetery.

That's when the trouble began. Within a few weeks, people from all over town came to the Rabbi of Crakow complaining that they had no means of support. "What did you live off till now?" he asked.

"We're not sure, but somehow we had food delivered and money sent to us under all types of strange pretexts. But now," they cried, " it has all stopped."

Carefully, the Rabbi traced each one's steps to the days preceding his good fortune. Each individual had been desperate for money and had tried to get something from the dastardly miser Yossele. Each one claimed that he was roughly shown the door with a few *zlotys* — and then in one or two weeks things began to change. Together with the Rabbi, the townsfolk realized that their first and partial glimpse of Yossele was all that remained in their minds. They had labeled him a miser and left his home dejected. It was not until after his death that they realized that Yossele the Miser was really Yossele the Holy Miser, benefactor of Crakow.

According to the commentaries, Bilaam knew that the power of his curses would only take effect by finding a small breach in the beauty of Israel — a breach that he could expand with the power of his evil eye. He looked at all of Israel and could not find any flaw to amplify and use as an opening for a curse.

Balak advised him to use another ploy, making a suggestion that would be followed for generations by all detractors of the Jews. "Only look at them," Balak said, "from a partial perspective. Go up to the side of the mountain. You shall see their edge and not all of them — and you will curse them for me from there" (cf. *Numbers* 23:13).

Balak told Bilaam to concentrate on some negative aspects of the people, for it is unfortunately possible to find a few exceptions among this most ethical and moral nation. There are indeed those detractors who stand on the side of the mountain and take a partial view. They talk about Jews who may be accused of crimes or improprieties. They dissect individuals and embellish what they perceive as character flaws or personal faults as if such flaws represent the entire nation. And then they shout their curses.

But Bilaam could not find the breach that he was looking for. Because Israel, as a nation, as well as each individual Jew, cannot be judged by anything less than the total picture — for we are all one.

PARSHAS PINCHAS

✍ Peace Through Strength

*Y*ou wouldn't buy a tone-deaf child a Stradivarius. Nor would you give a pair of ballet slippers to a girl with two left feet. Normally, parents try to enhance budding skills in their children while simultaneously realizing that it is futile to direct a child to pursue a vocation for which he has no talent or motivation. The *Talmud*, in fact, follows that reasoning. It advises that those with blood lust become ritual slaughterers, directing their violence toward meat instead of people. In this *parsha*, however, an act of justified violence is rewarded with a gift — a very special gift. The gift of *shalom* — peace. Why?

The previous portion ends as Zimri, a Jewish prince from the tribe of Shimon, flagrantly committed a lewd act with a Midianite princess in front of a multitude of Jews. Moses wept, and Ahron stood in disbelief. And Hashem looked on in anger.

A plague broke out, and Jews began dying. In the midst of the confusion, Pinchas, a *zealot* who was Ahron's grandson and himself a descendant of Midianite *geirim* (converts), grabbed a spear and killed Zimri and his partner simultaneously. Immediately, the plague ceased and tranquillity was restored.

In this portion, Pinchas is praised as a man who calmed the wrath of *Hashem* and is rewarded with both the priesthood and the blessing of eternal peace. But why is this zealot considered the "prince of peace?" Didn't he murder two people? Shouldn't he have been awarded a position of might? Perhaps he should have been appointed a general or a police captain instead?

Some years ago, a madman shot 19 people on a Long Island Railroad train. Three heroic individuals managed to subdue him and stop the carnage. They were lauded throughout the community. Had one of them had a spear and killed the murderer, he would have been no less a hero — perhaps even a greater one.

In this world, we see only the physical realities of danger — and we believe that if danger is imminently approaching us, it must be stopped by all means possible, even force. Yet, when there is a spiritual attack, we cower. Often we say it's none of our business — we can't get involved. Pinchas, however, saw the *spiritual* threat as clearly as the passengers on the 5:33 to Hicksville, Long Island saw the physical threat. He saw spiritual missiles flying from the licentious act of Zimri, killing thousands by way of a plague. Pinchas' act stopped the plague — a swift answer from a holy Jew who could not bear to see a madman spiritually shooting his brothers and sisters.

━━✦━━

After the British government issued the infamous White Paper in 1939, it was virtually impossible for a Jew to enter Palestine without a substantial cash reserve to prove that he was not indigent. At that time, Rabbi Yosef Farber, a *rosh yeshiva* and renowned European Torah scholar, was in New York trying to obtain the necessary visas which would allow his family, trapped in Europe, to emigrate to the Holy Land. The prerequisite, however, was to have $5,000 — a massive sum in those days — in a bank account.

Irving Bunim, one of America's foremost rescue workers, saw the plight of Rabbi Farber and gave him $5,000 to deposit in a bank. Although he was hassled by the British consulate in America, Rabbi Farber convinced them that he was a business associate of Mr. Bunim's and the money was actually his. The next step was simple — all Rabbi Farber had to do was to get the visa through the Jewish Agency.

Rabbi Farber's heart filled with joy as he entered the huge office with the enormous show window on Fifth Avenue. "Rabbi Farber, where in the world did you come up with so much money?" the surprised Dr. Tannenbaum asked. Rabbi Farber smiled broadly at the powerful American Zionist movement leader as he told him that Bunim had helped with some *tunkel-munkel* (hanky panky).

Enraged, Tannenbaum shouted, "Tell Bunim we don't do *tunkel-munkel* here! This is the government."

With tears in his eyes, Rabbi Farber returned to Mr. Bunim and told him what happened. Immediately, Irving Bunim got on the phone with the head of the Religious Zionists of America and the editor of the largest Yiddish daily. "I'll meet you for lunch tomorrow." He did not explain the purpose of the meeting, but Mr. Bunim made it very clear to them that they both must be there.

At the meeting, Mr. Bunim, a normally temperate businessman, told them of the plight of Rabbi Farber. He then unwrapped a huge rock. "Tomorrow," Bunim announced, "I am going to the giant show-window of the Jewish Agency, and I am going to smash it with this rock. I will be arrested, *The New York Times* will cover the spectacular story, and I will tell the world how our Agency's formalities helped in the murder of an illustrious family."

As the two men showed signs of disbelief, Bunim shouted, "If you don't believe me, I swear by my share in the World-To-Come!"

Suffice it to say that Rabbi Farber's entire family received the visas and was spared.

Pinchas had a very clear vision of love for Jews. It was a vision of peace. However, he saw Zimri's action the same way the LIRR passengers saw bullets. Pinchas saw spiritual bullets being sprayed at innocent bystanders. And he reacted — not because of his hate for Zimri, but because of his desire to save Jewish spirituality and Jewish lives.

We often are blinded by the niceties of social etiquette that prevent us from standing up and saying a strong word in the face of sin. Perhaps our reticence stems from the fact that we don't recognize sin's impact. If we understood the ramifications as Pinchas did, we'd also threaten to hurl rocks through windows. We would do so not out of anger or frustration, but for the sake of love and peace. Hashem saw that great talent in Pinchas and gave him the reward that was most fitting — the prize of peace.

PARSHAS MATOS

✐ A Bridge to Nowhere

---

oshe had been the consummate conciliator for 40 years. At the time of the sin of the Golden Calf, when he appeased Hashem, and through the many ordeals during the Jewish nation's desert sojourn, he was constantly an advocate for his people. In this *parsha*, however, Moshe reacted differently to what appears to be a simple request.

The children of Gad and Reuvain came to Moshe with a simple request. They were shepherds and did not want to cross the Jordan River, claiming that the land on the east bank of the river was better for grazing. They would rather stay on the east bank of the Jordan River while their brothers would cross into Canaan.

Yet, before they had a chance to present the logistics of the proposal, Moshe unleashed a virtual tirade at them. For 10 verses, more than any other single rebuke in the Torah, Moshe chastised them, for abandoning the other tribes who would have to conquer the land. He said that their request was subversive and would dissuade others from crossing the Jordan. Moshe then reiterated the fateful episode of the spies and their slander of the Land of Israel. He recounted the wrath of Hashem and detailed the suffering of Israel because of that sin. Finally, Moshe compared the representatives who requested to remain on the east bank to those terrible spies claiming that Gad and Reuvain "have risen in their place to add more to the burning wrath of Hashem against Israel" *(Numbers 32:6-16)*.

It is difficult to understand why Moshe, normally so patient and understanding even during the most difficult times, became so incensed at this request. Obviously, Moshe's actions are a lesson. What is it?

David was driving to the Catskills for *Shabbos* but he had set out from his Manhattan office with hardly enough time to make the trip before sundown. Traffic was backed up on the Major Deegan, and crossing the Hudson via the George Washington Bridge seemed an almost impossible task. Mid-span, after sitting nearly an hour in stop-and-go traffic, he realized that the red orb in the sky was about to sink below the horizon. David had never desecrated *Shabbos* before and traffic on the George Washington Bridge was not going to make him violate *Shabbos* now. In a panic, he pulled his car as close as he could to the guard rail, left the keys under the visor, removed his wallet and hid it together with his personal effects, and hoped for the best. At worst, the car would be stolen. Maybe the police would get to it first and tow it.

Feeling a little guilty about adding to the traffic delays on the bridge, David left his car, flashers blinking, and walked back toward New York City where he decided to spend *Shabbos* with a friend who lived in nearby Washington Heights.

He returned to the bridge Saturday night, and his car was nowhere to be seen. David went straight to a police station and asked for the desk officer. "Did anyone see the gray Honda that was on the George Washington Bridge on Friday night?" he asked.

The officer's eyes widened. "You mean the car with the keys under the visor?"

David nodded.

"Franky, get over here," the cop yelled to a friend. Listen to this!"

A couple of officers moved closer to David.

The sergeant raised his voice. "You mean the Honda with the flashers on?"

Again David nodded, this time more nervously.

"You mean the Honda with the wallet with close to $500 dollars left under the front seat!" he shouted. "*Was that your car?*"

David shook his head meekly. "Yes, officer, that's my car. Where is it?"

"Where is it?" mocked the officer. *"Where is it?* Do you know how many divers we have looking for your body in the Hudson?"

❧

Moshe understood that the worst of all sins is not what one does privately in his heart or in his home, but rather how his actions affect the spirit of others. Often, one's self-interest overshadows any thought of how his conduct will affect others. The children of Gad and Reuvain had a personal issue: they did not want to cross the Jordan River because they wanted to graze in greener pastures. Yet they did not consider what effect their request might have on an entire nation. They did not take into account the severe ramifications their actions might have had on the morale of hundreds of thousands of enthusiastic people wanting to enter the Holy Land.

In our lives — at home and at work — not everything that we do, say, or act upon may be interpreted with the same intent that motivated the action. And sometimes those misinterpretations can have devastating effects on morale, attitude, and feeling. We may refuse to cross a river for a matter of convenience. Others, however, may see our refusal as a calamity. Our job is to be conscious that everything we do affects not only ourselves but also many other people as well.

PARSHAS MASEI

➤ Having a Ball...and Chain

*T*here is a fascinating law in this *parsha*. The Torah states that one who kills accidentally must be banished to an *ir miklat*, a city of refuge. The Torah refers to an accident that is tinged with a bit of negligence, neither a total mishap nor a death tainted with intent. And the cities of refuge were the home of the *Levites*, whose life's mission was service to others. Thus the perpetrator would witness a lesson in care and concern during his stay, a lesson which would hopefully penetrate — even elevate — his soul.

Then the Torah presents the very unique terms granting a killer's release from the *ir miklat*. He was to stay until the *Kohen Gadol* (High Priest) died. Of course, the reaction of his *Levite* neighbors, who were the protégés of the *Kohen Gadol* mourning the loss of their beloved leader, would temper the murderer's joy of freedom and put it in perspective. Indeed, it would be almost impossible to feel exuberant about one's own release among the thousands of residents mourning their leader — a final lesson before resuming a new life in society.

But the Torah identifies the *Kohen Gadol*, whose death results in the killer's release, in a strange way. "He (the killer) shall remain in it (the city of refuge) until the passing of the *Kohen Gadol* whom *he* anointed"(*Numbers* 35:25). The Talmud in *Makos* is baffled by the words *whom he anointed*. It somewhat implies that the killer was involved with the *Kohen's* anointing – and *that* just cannot be. After all, wasn't the *Kohen* anointed well in advance of the fatal accident that led to the killer's incarceration?

The Talmud answers: True; however, this verse implies that if, after the time of the accident but before its judicial resolution, a new *Kohen Gadol* is anointed, then the killer only is released after the new *Kohen's* death.

The Talmud asks why. This new *Kohen Gadol* was not around during the accident. True, he was appointed before the verdict, but he was appointed after the *death* occurred. Why is he somehow involved in the verdict of the accused? Why is *his* death the redeeming factor for the accused? Why is he punished? The Talmud answers that if there were a trial during the new *Kohen Gadol's* tenure, he should have prayed for the welfare of the accused. He should have interceded and prayed in order to mitigate a verdict of exile. Therefore, if the verdict was rendered during *his* tenure, then the man is released with *his* death.

It is still quite difficult to understand. How is an incoming *Kohen Gadol*, during the most exciting and prestigious period of his career to be expected to worry about the verdict of a man he has never heard of, accused of manslaughter?

Rabbi Chaim Kanievski, of B'nei Berak, Israel, the son of the Steipler Gaon, of blessed memory, is known for his amazing breadth of Torah knowledge paralleled only by his great diligence in Torah study. Since the passing of his father more than a decade ago, people from all walks of life line up in front of his home seeking answers to complex Torah and personal questions. But his greatness and wisdom were known to hundreds in the yeshiva world for many years.

Many years ago, as a student in the Ponovez Yeshiva, I heard an amazing story. A young man came to Reb Chaim with a long list of questions. Reb Chaim seemed a bit preoccupied, but the visitor insisted on asking the questions, to which Reb Chaim responded, one by one.

Suddenly, Reb Chaim began freshening himself up and then donned a recently pressed *kapote* and new hat. He asked the young man's indulgence — he had to go somewhere, but allowed the visitor to accompany him. The younger man complied, peppering him with questions the entire time they walked together.

They walked a few blocks until they reached a wedding hall. Upon entering, Reb Chaim embraced the groom with a warm hug and kiss and apologized for the delay. Reb Chaim sat himself among the prestigious *rabbonim* (rabbis) who graced the dais as they prepared the marriage documents. The persistent questioner was almost oblivious to the scene and continued to ask more questions, and, amazingly, he elicited responses. Reb Chaim tried to juggle the needs of the groom while trying to accommodate the visitor who had besieged him with problems.

But the persistent questioner received the shock of his life when the music began, heralding the march to the *badekin*, where the groom, flanked by his father and father-in-law, meets the bride and covers her face with the veil. The groom rose from his seat, and immediately his future father-in-law took hold of his arm. The groom's father took hold of the other arm. But before he did so, the groom's father turned around and apologized to the stranger whom he had been talking to for the last hour or so. He said that he would be unable to help him until after the ceremony. And then Rabbi Kanievski nodded Mazel Tov to the hundreds of well-wishers and began the procession to his own son's wedding!

The Torah tells us that the *Kohen Gadol*-elect, waiting to be anointed to the most spiritual position in Judaism, has a responsibility to worry about the welfare of the common man — even one accused of manslaughter. The *Kohen Gadol* should worry about the accused's welfare and the verdict on his life. For there is no greater inauguration to the responsibilities of priesthood than the concern for every single one of us. Because you can't have a ball when someone else is chained.

ספר דברים

The Book of Deuteronomy

PARSHAS DEVORIM

⮞ A Meaningful Approach

*F*orty years of desert wanderings were coming to a close. Moshe knew that his end was near and wanted to leave the Children of Israel with parting words that were filled with love, direction, guidance, and admonition.

Addressing the Jewish nation, he discussed many of the events of the previous four decades, both the triumphs and the tragedies. Though he did not mince words, there were many details that Moshe added in his review that shed additional light on previously related incidents.

One incident in particular was that of the *meraglim*, the spies, who returned to the Jewish camp from Canaan with horrific tales and predictions of sure defeat. Moshe recounted: "All of you approached me, saying, 'let us send spies and they shall seek the land'" (*Deuteronomy* 1:22). Rashi commented on the words "all of you." "In confusion, the young pushed the old," Rashi explains, "and the elders pushed ahead of the leaders." Rashi adds that at the giving of the Torah, however, the elders and the youth came in an orderly fashion to present their needs. But why does it matter how the request was presented? In addition, why does Rashi deem it necessary to contrast this poor conduct with the proper decorum that occurred at the giving of the Torah?

⮞⮜

During the first weeks of the American Civil War, newspaper editorials from across the nation were filled with a plethora of criticisms, advice, and second-guessing of President Lincoln's handling of the widening conflict. Eventually, the editors asked for a meeting with the President, which he granted.

During the meeting, each editor interrupted the other with ideas, suggestions, and posturing.

Suddenly, Mr. Lincoln stood up. "Gentlemen," he exclaimed "this discussion reminds me of the story of the traveler whose carriage wheel broke in the middle of a thunderstorm during the black of night. The rain was pouring, the thunder was booming, and the carriage was sinking, as the man desperately tried to fix the wheel. He groped and grappled in the wet darkness, looking for a solution to his problem.

"Suddenly, a magnificent bolt of lightning lit the countryside like daylight. Seconds later, the ground shook from a clap of thunder that reverberated for miles with a deafening boom.

"The hapless traveler looked toward Heaven and tearfully pleaded with his Creator. 'Lord,' he begged, 'is it possible to provide a little more light and a little less noise?'"

~~~

A few years before his passing, my grandfather, Rabbi Yaakov Kamenetzky, of blessed memory, visited Israel and was asked to deliver a *shiur* (lecture) in a prominent yeshiva on a difficult Talmudic passage.

Upon his arrival at the yeshiva, he was shocked to see hordes of students and outsiders clamoring to get front-row seats in order to hear his lecture. There was quite a bit of pushing and shoving; after all, at the time Reb Yaakov was the world's oldest living Talmudic sage, and this lecture was an unprecedented privilege for the throngs who entered the yeshiva to get a glimpse of the Torah giant and listen to the wisdom he was about to offer. Yet it was difficult for him to approach the lectern because of the chaos.

Indeed, the goings-on did not please him. So Reb Yaakov discarded his planned lecture and instead posed the following question to the students: "In *Parshas Shelach*, the portion of the spies, the Torah tells us that each *shevet* (tribe) sent one spy. In fact, the Torah lists each spy according to his tribe. Yet unlike the ordinary enumeration of the tribes, this one is quite different. It is out of order. The Torah begins by listing the first four tribes in order of birth, but then jumps to Ephraim, who was the youngest, then to Benyamin, then back to Menashe. Dan and Asher follow, with the tribes of Naftali and Gad ensuing. Many commentaries struggle to make some semblance of order out of this seeming hodgepodge of tribes. It is very strange indeed.

"But," Reb Yaakov explained as he gazed with disappointment upon the unruly crowd, "perhaps Rashi in *Devorim* resolves the reason for the staggered enumeration. The reason they are mentioned out of order is simply because there was no order! The young pushed the old out of the way and moved ahead to say their piece. And from that moment, the mission was doomed."

Many of us have ideas and opinions. As we see in this *parsha*, the manner in which they are presented may have as much impact on their success as the ideas themselves.

PARSHAS VOESCHANAN

~ Mortal Torah

*I*t is said with a combination of passionate joy and admiring wonder. As the Torah is raised for all to see, the congregants point to it and recite a verse from this *parsha*, "*V'zos haTorah asher som Moshe...*" "This is the Torah that Moshe presented before the Children of Israel" (*Deuteronomy* 4:44). It would seem that this verse refers to the deep and beautiful laws that inspire the same awe as the sight of the Torah scroll itself unfurled in all its glory. It doesn't.

In fact, the words now used to proclaim the glory of the Torah in its entirety are placed directly after a section of the Torah we would rather not have appear. The words "*v'zos haTorah*" — "this is the Torah" — follow the laws of the cities of refuge. People convicted of negligent manslaughter, or who are awaiting trial for that crime, must stay in specially designated cities until the *Kohen Gadol* (high priest) dies.

The cities of refuge were strategically located, and the Torah reviews both the entry qualifications and the terms of inhabitance. We Jews are certainly not proud of killers, yet we obviously must deal with them. The question is, however, why are the words, "this is the Torah," which seem to embody the very essence of our code of life, placed in proximity to laws that regulate our lowest point?

Rashi comments on this juxtaposition, stating that the words refer to an ensuing portion which recounts the Sinai experience and receiving the Ten Commandments. Ramban explains that after Moshe's admonition of the people, he once again resumed discussing the laws with them. I would like to take a more homiletic approach.

In the early 1900s, a rabbi who lived in the tenements of Manhattan's Lower East Side had to attend a city function at which a notoriously anti-Semitic Episcopalian Minister was also present.

The minister turned to the rabbi and with a sinister smile remarked, "What a coincidence! It was just last night that I dreamt I was in Jewish heaven."

"Jewish heaven?" inquired the rabbi. "What is it like in Jewish heaven?"

"Oh!" the minister replied, "in Jewish heaven the streets were filled with Jews. Children, their faces dirty, shirts untucked, and clothes unpressed, were playing in the dirt. Women were haggling with fish-vendors, as Jewish beggars tried to interrupt, asking for handouts. The clotheslines stretched across the roads, and water from the dripping wash mixed with the dust below adding more mud to the existing mess on the ground. And of course," the minister added with a vicious laugh, "rabbis were running back and forth with large Talmudic volumes tucked under their arms!"

The rabbi pursed his lips and then replied, "That is truly amazing. You see, I dreamt last night that I was in Episcopalian heaven."

"Really?" the minister asked. "And pray tell me what was it like in Episcopalian heaven?"

"It was magnificent," the rabbi smiled. "The streets shone as if they had recently been washed. The homes were exquisitely lined up in perfect symmetry, each with a small garden that had beautiful flowers and a perfectly manicured lawn. All the buildings were freshly painted, and they sparkled in the sunlight!"

The minister beamed. "And what about the people?" he questioned. "Tell me about the people!"

The rabbi smiled, looked the minister right in the eye, and tersely stated, "There were no people."

By placing the words "this is the Torah that Moshe present-ed" directly after the laws of the cities of refuge, the Torah sends a message that it does not evade guiding the Jewish people through every aspect of life. Whether the Torah is commanding the laws of priestly blessings, sharing the Passover story, or reha-bilitating a man who accidentally killed another, it presents them equally and proclaims them proudly as such. We don't ignore our misfortunes or hide them as if they do not exist. The laws concerning thievery and murder are as much a part of the Torah as the perpetrators are part of society, and we don't hide the unfortunate and wrongdoers from our existence. And when the Torah deals with them, it boldly states that this, too, is the Torah that Moshe placed before the Children of Israel.

PARSHAS EKEV

⌇ On Cue

Not often does God Almighty tell anybody to leave Him alone. But then again, Moshe wasn't anybody.

In this *parsha*, Moshe recounts the sad tale of the Golden Calf. Moshe had promised to return from Mount Sinai 40 days after receiving the Torah, but the Jews misjudged. According to their calculations he was late. Fearing that Moshe would never return from his celestial mission, the Jews made themselves a golden calf and worshipped it while proclaiming, "This is your god O Israel, that took you out of Egypt." Obviously, the calculations and miscalculations of the Jewish People are not as simple as they appear on the surface. That, however, is an entirely different issue.

As part of the aftermath of the calamity of the Golden Calf, Hashem wanted to destroy the Jewish Nation and rebuild a new one with Moshe as its patriarchal leader. "Release Me," God said, "and I will destroy them and build a new nation from you" (*Cf. Deuteronomy* 9:14). Immediately after the words "release Me," Moshe sprang into action. *Exodus* details how Moshe pleaded, appealed, and reasoned with Hashem, using a multitude of persuasive arguments that calmed His wrath. The Jews were spared.

What is troubling, is Moshe's seeming *chutzpah*? Didn't Hashem specifically tell him, "leave Me alone?" What prompted him to have the courage to defy a direct command of Hashem?

❧

Herbert Tenzer was a distinguished Congressman from New York who served in the 1960s. More important, he was an observant Jew who was a proud activist and instrumental in providing relief for many

Holocaust survivors. A few months before his passing, he related to me the following story:

The energetic and often outspoken Rabbi Eliezer Silver of Cincinnati, Ohio, was a prominent force in the Vaad Hatzalah Rescue Committee who worked tirelessly throughout the terrible war years and their aftermath to save and then place the victims of Nazi depravity. In addition to his prominence in the Jewish world, Rabbi Silver enjoyed a personal relationship with the very powerful Senator Robert Taft of Ohio.

One time, Rabbi Silver had a very difficult request that required much political pressure and persuasion to accomplish. As such, he asked Mr. Tenzer to accompany him to the Senator.

"Shenator Taft!" Rabbi Silver exclaimed, in his distinct Lithuanian accent in which the "s" sounded as "sh," combined with a high-pitched intoning of emotions. "I have a very important and difficult requesht!"

Rabbi Silver went on to plead his case about obtaining a certain number of visas for some refugees who may not have met all the criteria. Senator Taft looked nonchalant and non-committal, thought for a while, then grimaced while he slowly and carefully prolonged his response. "It would be arduous and burdensome," he began, "but technically," he continued, implying that he was not the least bit anxious to get his hands dirty, "it can be done."

But Rabbi Silver did not hear anything except the last four words.

"IT CAN BE DONE?" he shouted with joy. "SHO DO IT!"

Needless to say, the stunned Senator got to work immediately and obtained the visas for the beleaguered Jews.

～✦～

Moshe heard one line from Hashem, "If you leave Me alone, I will destroy them." That was his cue. The Talmud in *Berachos* explains that those words mobilized Moshe: He knew that it all depended on him. The only way Hashem would destroy His people was if Moshe left Him alone. And he didn't. Moshe pleaded with the Almighty, and we were spared.

A Rebbe of mine once quoted legendary slugger Ted Williams, the last baseball player to achieve a batting average of over .400: "Every player gets one pitch that he definitely can hit. To hit .400, don't miss that pitch." Instead of recoiling at the words "release me" or "leave me be," Moshe saw his pitch. And he hit it awfully hard.

In life there are many cues. In this *parsha* Moshe taught his nation that when you get your cue, don't miss it. Even if it takes a little *chutzpah*.

PARSHAS RE'EH

✐ *Giving Personally*

*I*n this *parsha* the Torah teaches about charity. Not only does it tell *who* should give, it also tells *how* to give. And it does so in an uncharacteristic and seemingly repetitive fashion.

"If there shall be an impoverished person from among you or any of your brethren in your cities ... you shall not harden your heart or close your hand against your destitute brother... Rather you shall surely give him, and you shall not harden your heart when you give him" (*Deuteronomy* 15:7-10).

The repetitive expression and emphasis on the word *him* is curious. "You shall surely give him and not feel bad" would suffice. Why is the phrase "when you give *him*" (*Deuteronomy* 15:10) necessary? The Torah is referring to the person to whom you have given. It tells us not to feel bad about giving charity. Why the extra phrase about the recipient?

➤➤➤

Rabbi Yosef Dov Soleveitchik, the Rav of Brisk, was revered throughout Europe as a great scholar and Talmudic sage. Yet one aspect of his character was known to shine even brighter than his scholarship — his humility.

Once, he stopped by an inn in the middle of a freezing night and asked for lodging. He had no entourage with him, and the innkeeper treated him with abuse. Rabbi Soleveitchik did not disclose who he was, and after pleading with the innkeeper, Rabbi Soloveitchik was allowed to sleep on the floor near a stove. The innkeeper, thinking that the man was a poor beggar, did not even offer him any food — and in fact refused to give him more than a little bread and water for which Rabbi Soleveitchik was willing to pay.

The next morning Rabbi Soleveitchik did not see the shocked expression on the face of the innkeeper when a few of the town notables came to the inn. "We understand that the Brisker Rav was passing through town," they said. "Is it possible that he came by your inn last night?"

At first, the innkeeper dismissed the question — until the Rav appeared and the group greeted him warmly. In a few minutes the town dignitaries all converged on the inn, with their students and children standing in line to greet the great sage.

Terribly embarrassed, the innkeeper, who realized that he had berated and humiliated a leading Torah figure, begged forgiveness from the Rav.

"Rebbe," he cried, "I am terribly sorry. I had no idea that you were the Brisker Rav. Please forgive me."

The Rav replied, "I would love to, but, you see, that would be impossible."

"But why?" the shocked owner asked.

"You see," the sage explained, "you are coming to ask forgiveness from the Brisker Rav. That is not whom you insulted. You debased a simple Jew who came for lodging — and he is no longer here to forgive you."

⚡

The Torah explains that in essence there are two parties involved in *tzedaka* (charity) — the patron and the recipient. Often the giver is detached from the recipient; he wants to give but has no concern for the receiver. The giver may even have disdain for the person at the door, but the *mitzvah* of *tzedaka* overrides his pre-judgment and he gives a contribution. So the Torah stresses the words "do not feel badly in your heart when you give to him" to teach us an important lesson.

In addition to the *mitzvah* of giving, one should identify with the recipient, too. Know the true situation of the person to whom you are giving. Understand what you are giving for. Be sure that when you give you should not feel bad in your heart.

The Torah recognizes that the simplest beggar is someone worthy enough to be mentioned twice: "Surely give *him*; do not feel bad in your heart when you give *him*." If the Torah is careful enough to classify the beggar as an individual who transcends a generic recipient, and transforms him into a personal beneficiary, then surely he is worthy of recognition by all of us.

PARSHAS SHOFTIM

✦ Branches of the Judiciary

*J*uxtapositions. The Talmud analyzes them and expounds upon them. After all, every word of the Torah is as important as the next, and the positioning of each law in the Heavenly ordained book bears great symbolism, if not outright *halachic* (legal) implication.

Perhaps that is the reason that our sages expounded upon a very interesting juxtaposition in this portion.

This *parsha* is named *Shoftim* — Judges. That is exactly what it begins with, commanding the Jewish people to appoint judges. They should be honest, upright, and unwavering. They may not take any form of bribery, as the Torah unequivocally states that even the most brilliant and pious soul will be blinded and perverted by bribes. Conspicuously placed next to these laws is the prohibition against planting *asheira* trees. While the *asheira* tree appeared the same as any other tree, it served another purpose: it was worshipped as an idol.

Those two sections adjoin and the Talmud in Tractate *Sanhedrin* explains that the Torah is making a stark comparison. "Anyone who appoints an unworthy judge is as if he planted the idolatrous *asheira* tree in his midst."

The obvious question is that although both acts are sinful, there must be a greater reason they are placed together other than the fact that they both are wrong. What is the connection?

There was a period in the 1970s when a group of rogues was smuggling valuables in *tefillin* (phylacteries) and other religious articles that usually are not subject to customs inspection. Often, the smugglers sent these religious articles with unsuspecting Jews, asking them to deliver the materials to locations near the Jews' final destinations.

When United States customs officials got wind of this scheme, they asked a few religiously observant Jewish agents to help crack the ring. In addition to preserving the sanctity of the religious items, the customs authorities felt that the strictly religious agents would best be able to separate knowing accomplices from unsuspecting participants who had been duped into thinking they were actually performing a *mitzvah*.

The Jewish customs agent in charge of the operation decided to confer with my grandfather, Rabbi Yaakov Kamenetzky, on this matter. Though Reb Yaakov's advice on how to break the ring remains confidential, he told me how the severity of the crime was compounded by its use of religious items.

"Smuggling diamonds in *tefillin*," my grandfather explained, "is equivalent to raising a white flag, approaching the enemy lines as if to surrender, and then lobbing a grenade. That soldier has not only perpetrated a fraud on his comrades and victors, he has also betrayed a symbol of civilization. With one devious act, he has destroyed a trusted symbol for eternity — forever endangering the lives of countless soldiers for years to come.

"These thieves, by taking a sacrosanct symbol and using it as a vehicle for a crime, are destroying the eternal sanctity and symbolism of a sacred object. Their evil actions may cause irreparable damage to countless honest religious people. These rogues must be stopped by any means possible," he said.

～✳～

Rabbi Chaim Soleveitchik explained the comparison of the *asheira* tree to a corrupt judge: an *asheira* tree is very deceiving. While it is as beautiful as any other tree, man has turned its natural aesthetic beauty into a vehicle for blasphemy. "A judge," Rabbi Soleveitchik explained, "also has many aesthetic attributes. He may have an honest appearance, even a regal demeanor. In fact, he could wear a long *kapote* (frock coat) and have a flowing beard. His very image exudes traits that personify honesty, integrity, and morality. However, if he is inherently dishonest, then he is no better than a lovely tree whose sole purpose is to promote a heretical ritual of idolatry."

The judge and the tree may both look appealing and could be used as vehicles to promote God's glory, but in these cases they are not. In fact, quite the opposite: these formerly beautiful objects now bring disgrace to the Creator.

And so the Torah tells us that while trees may have outer beauty, but cannot be unequivocally classified as being an ever-lasting testimony to Hashem's glory, likewise a judge whose demeanor may be noble may nevertheless be a source of deception who can bring disgrace to an entire nation. Therefore, both are presented together — for both must be shunned. And although both may have beautiful external appearances, a beautiful appearing tree and a distinguished looking judge may both have evil roots.

PARSHAS
KI SAYTZAY

➤ Soup Opera

*L*ove. It is a word that is supposed to explain the feelings that bind two individuals, parent and child, man and wife, God and *His* creations. The love between a man and his wife is the constant symbol used in Shlomo *HaMelech's Shir Hashirim* (Song of Songs) to declare the unshakable love God has for His nation.

But divorce is also a fact of life and in this *parsha* the Torah, albeit very succinctly, discusses the method of divorce. It also tells us why marriages end. "It will be if she does not find favor in his eyes for he found in her an *ervas davar* then he may write a divorce..." (*Deuteronomy* 24:1). The *Mishna* in Tractate *Gittin* discusses the meaning of *ervas davar* in different ways. Bais Shammai, who is known for following a strict opinion in most matters, says that divorce should only occur over a matter of immorality. Bais Hillel says, that divorce is permitted "even if she burns his soup." And Rabbi Akiva, whose devotion and gratitude to his wife is legendary, says that "even if he finds a nicer woman, (he may divorce)."

It is most difficult to understand the *Mishna*. It seems to run counter to of every Talmudic teaching. How do Bais Hillel, those who spoke of loving peace and pursuing peace, say that one may get divorced over burned soup? Rabbi Akiva once pointed to his wife in front of 24,000 students and announced, "Whatever I have and whatever you have, it is all due to her." How could he then say that one could get divorced if he found a more lovely woman? It seems very puzzling!

My father, Rabbi Binyomin Kamenetzky, Rosh Yeshiva of the Yeshiva of South Shore, once told me a wonderful story: Reb Dovid was happily married to his dear and loving wife, Chayka, for nearly half a century. Her sudden death cast him into a terrible depression for which there seemed to be almost no cure. His son, Moshe and daughter-in-law, Roizy, graciously invited him to stay at their home and share everything with them. Reb Dovid's daughter-in-law, cooked every meal for him, but Reb Dovid was never satisfied. No matter how deliciously prepared the meals were, he would sigh and mutter to himself, loud enough for his son to hear, "this was not the way Momma made the soup."

Roizy pored over her mother-in-law's old recipe books and tried to re-create the delicious taste for which her father-in-law longed. But Reb Dovid never was pleased.

One day, while the soup was cooking, Reb Dovid's grandchild fell outside. In her haste to get to the child, Roizy poured almost the entire pepper shaker into the soup. Additionly, by the time the child was washed and bandaged, the soup was totally burned!

There was nothing for Reb Dovid's daughter to do but serve the heavily spiced, burnt soup.

She watched in despair as her elderly father-in-law brought the soup to his lips. This time he would probably more than mumble a complaint. But it was not to be. A wide smile broke across Reb Dovid's face. "Delicious my dear Roizy," said Reb Dovid with a tear in his eye. "Absolutely delicious! This is exactly how Momma made the soup!"

My grandfather, Rabbi Yaakov Kamenetzky, in his *sefer Emes L'Yaakov* explains the *Mishna* in an amazing fashion: it is giving us a sign, when a marriage is in a state of disrepair. If a man tastes burnt soup that his loving wife cooked and he is repulsed, then he is missing the love that the Torah requires. Rabbi Akiva, who was separated from his wife for 24 years while he studied Torah, declared that if a man finds a woman whom he thinks is better, then his marriage needs scrutiny! Because a husband must think that there is nothing tastier than what his wife prepared, and that there is no one more lovely than the woman he married.

Reb Aryeh Levin, the *Tzadik* of Jerusalem, once entered a doctor's office with his wife and spoke on behalf of both of them. "Her leg hurts us," he said. This simple remark epitomizes the desired relationship between husband and wife.

The *Mishna* is *not* defining how to get divorced. That is easy. It is teaching us an attitude that defines love. Because love is a lot more than not having to say I'm sorry. It's always believing that the soup is delicious — even if it is burnt.

PARSHAS
KI SAVO

✐ *Fine Print*

*T*here is nothing more disheartening than a curse. And this
week the Torah singles out specific violations that are worthy
of the epithet, "cursed is he who " The Torah tells us that the
nation was divided into two parts. Six tribes stood on Mount
Grizim, and the rest stood on Mount Ebal. The Levites began to
specify the sins that the Torah prefaced with the harsh warning,
"accursed is one who," and the nation would respond amen.
Included among the terrible crimes are one who moves his
neighbors' boundary and one who misleads a blind man on the
road. The curses also include carnal sins and striking a person
covertly *(Deuteronomy 27:12-25)*. In fact, almost each curse is
related to a sin that entails some degree of surreptitiousness. All
except the final curse, "Accursed is the one who does not uphold
the words of this Torah to perform them" *(Deuteronomy 27:26)*.
Rashi explains the last admonition as a general warning to heed
all the laws in the Torah lest one suffer the curses. The Ramban,
however, softens Rashi's severe interpretation. He explains that
the curse is not directed toward one who actually commits a sin,
but rather at those who scoff at the validity of the Torah's laws.

Following his simple explanation, the Ramban writes something startling: "It appears to me that the words 'accursed is the
one who does not uphold the words of the Torah' refers to one
who is called upon to do the *hagbah* ceremony in the synagogue
and does not unfurl the Torah wide enough for the congregation
to see the words."

For years I was terribly disturbed by that explanation. I could
not fathom the sense of comparison. How can the Ramban

equate one who does a poor *hagbah* with those who surreptitiously undermine the welfare of their neighbor or create clandestine instability within the family? How can we attribute the harsh words of *accursed* to one who does not have what it takes to do a proper *hagbah*?

On a whistle stop tour during his term in office, Calvin Coolidge's train stopped in St. Louis where a crowd of nearly 2,500 people gathered to hear him. He was sleeping in his railcar when the train stopped at the station and Colonel Starling, Coolidge's personal assistant and agent-in-charge, nudged him awake.

"Mr. President," he said while tapping him on the shoulder, "there are almost three thousand people who are waiting to hear you!"

The remarkably restrained Coolidge and the first lady stepped out onto the train's observation platform. The crowd applauded wildly. Then the local master of ceremonies called for silence. "The President is about to speak now!"

The President stood silently with a wide smile. He straightened his jacket and smoothed his hair and appeared very presidential. The crowd waited anxiously for him to begin his speech. The President waited, too. Just then, there was a hiss of air as the brakes were released and the train began pulling away from the station. The President, still smiling, raised his hand, waved, and spoke. He said, "Goodbye."

Perhaps the Ramban's message is more profound. When one displays the parchment of the Torah but does not sufficiently unfurl the columns, he deprives the congregation from seeing the true essence of Torah. He parades with a Torah scroll with the shiny handles and the traditional parchment. It looks beautiful, even majestic. It even looks very spiritual. And the crowd waits for the real context to be exhibited.

But if those columns are not unfurled for the congregation to read, the stark reality of God's command is hidden behind the splendor of the moment. Performing *hagbah* in this manner is effect almost equivalent to misleading the blind, secretly moving a neighbor's border, and making overt displays of honesty that are rife with deceit. For in reality a serious truth is being hidden underhandedly. And for that, the Ramban links him with the definitive consequences of those who morally deprave Torah ideals. Obviously, one who proudly unfurls the truth and tells the story as it appears is worthy of the greatest blessings offered in the Torah. For there is no greater blessing than the open honesty and true teaching of Hashem's will. However, lifting a Torah, unopened, in front of a waiting audience is nothing more than disappointing an excited crowd who are waiting for a substantive speech. You may be waving enthusiastically, but all you are saying is goodbye.

PARSHAS NITZAVIM

≈ *Spaced Out*

*T*he Torah, this portion tells us, is not in space. We do not have to travel to the heavens, or cross the seas, to learn it. Instead, it is close to our lips and our hearts to perform them (*Deuteronomy* 30:11-14). Though the Torah is not in the heavens, that is not always the case with Jews! We read in this *parsha* that sometimes the Jewish people will be so dispersed that "if your exiles are scattered at the ends of the heavens, Hashem will gather them from there" (*Deuteronomy* 30:4).

These verses present an amazing contrast. Though the Jewish people may be as far-flung as the heavens themselves, the Torah is always within our reach. Ultimately, however, both the distant Jew and the Torah he is meant to study and observe will be together.

Yet the meaning of this message is surely open to analysis. What does the Torah mean by telling us that it is not in heaven? We all know that. After all, aren't we reading and studying these verses at home, in the synagogue, here on earth?

Rashi explains that the Torah means to tell us that if it were actually in heaven we would have to find a way to retrieve it, bring it back to earth, and study it! Quite a prescient prediction of space travel! But if the quest for a possible cure for cancer or other scientific discoveries prompted a multi-billion-dollar space program with the goal to land on the moon, Mars, and other celestial neighbors, the quest for morality would certainly have propelled us there thousands of years prior!

Perhaps an old Jewish tale demonstrates how the Torah entreats us in a different vein.

The story is told of Reb Chaikel, a poor tailor from Lodz, who had a recurring dream. Each night, his father appeared to him and told him about a secret fortune. All Reb Chaikel had to do was travel to Vienna and visit the royal palace. Exactly 50 yards from the palace, his father explained, was an old oak tree. Under that tree, his father told him, lay a great treasure. If Reb Chaikel would dig under the tree, all his financial problems would be solved.

At first, Reb Chaikel ignored the dream, but it kept recurring night after night, and finally he felt compelled to travel to Vienna and seek his fortune.

He camped out near the palace and waited for an opportune moment to start excavating. At midnight on a moonless night, he stealthily crept up to the tree and began to dig. Scarcely had his shovel struck the ground when he felt a rough hand squeeze the back of his neck.

"Jew!" the palace guard shouted, "what on earth are you doing at midnight, 50 yards from the palace gates, shoveling dirt?"

Reb Chaikel had no choice but to tell him the story of the dream and the great fortune that lay beneath the oak tree. He even offered to split the booty, if only the guard would let him go.

"You idiot!" the guard laughed. "Everyone has dreams. In fact, I myself dreamt that if I would go to the city of Lodz in Poland, and dig in the basement of some Jewish tailor named Chaikel, I, too, would find a fortune! Hah! Now get lost!"

Legend has it that Reb Chaikel returned to Lodz, and after a little digging in his own home became a very wealthy man.

Sometimes, we view the Torah's goals as being far away in space! And we look at *mitzvos* as nearly impossible tasks that are as difficult to perform as landing on the moon. Sadly, they become hurdles that we find impossible to overcome — not even feasible to attempt. We think that to succeed we must travel to distant lands and perform incredible feats.

The Torah assures us twice that its strictures are well within our reach. A Jewish soul may be lost in space, but Hashem will find a way to bring it home. Whether through a chance meeting with an observant Jew in Thailand, or seated next to him on an airplane circling the Dallas airport, Hashem will find him. Then, the Torah promises us that its manual of practical observance is a lot more manageable than people may imagine. One may think it takes extensive efforts to master the Torah — to become something he imagines is way beyond his reach — but the Torah tells us this is not the case.

The Torah assures us that the Jewish spirit has an eternal bond with the Torah that was written to guide it. They are very similar and they are both within our reach. Neither of them is spaced out forever.

PARSHAS VAYELECH

➣ Lasting Impressions

*M*ost *mitzvos* in the Torah are prescribed for adults. Children are taught to follow the examples of their elders, who in turn have a responsibility to train them. However, except for a handful of *mitzvos*, such as circumcision and teaching Torah, none are directed specifically toward children.

In this *parsha*, however, the Torah openly instructs fathers to involve children, even toddlers, in the *mitzvah* of *hakhel*. Every seven years, at the close of the *shmita* cycle, on the first day of *Chol HaMoed Sukkos*, there is a gathering of the entire Jewish nation in Jerusalem. There, the King of Israel reads from *Deuteronomy* to the nation. Everyone is invited; no one should stay home. The Torah explicitly directs men, women, children, and even toddlers to make the trek to Jerusalem for this momentous occasion.

Indeed, this very infrequent event carried great significance for the Jewish nation. It was at this time that the King openly reaffirmed his faith in God, and a multitude of Jews joined to hear, once again, the edicts of the Torah.

So why bring the kids? Rashi quotes the Talmud in Tractate *Chagigah*: "And the children, why do they attend? To give reward to those who bring them!" This is difficult to understand. Did you ever go to a synagogue packed with babies, toddlers, and youngsters? Is that a conducive setting for the King of all Israel to read our most sacred covenant? Can you imagine how difficult it must have been to *schlep* the babies to Jerusalem, house and feed them, then have them sit through some hours-long reading of laws, admonishments, and prophecies that they could not possibly comprehend? And how does the Torah expect adults to hear the Torah's words and contemplate the King's charge during all this commotion?

❧

Rabbi Moshe Weinberger of Congregation Aish Kodesh, Woodmere, related a moving story that he heard from an elderly Lithuanian Jew. This man had survived the Holocaust, Siberia, and a myriad of painful experiences, all with his faith intact. As a young teenager, he was sent by his parents to learn at the yeshiva in Grodno, Poland, headed by the illustrious Torah sage, Rabbi Shimon Shkopf. This yeshiva was known to accept only the brightest students, therefore this young teen, who was average at best, worried that he would be summarily rejected. After three days of travel by train, carriage, and foot, he finally entered the portals of the yeshiva. Rabbi Shkopf personally greeted the young man and invited him to his home, but he could not help but notice how haggard the boy looked. Rabbi Shkopf then asked him from which city he came and surmised how difficult the journey must have been.

When the Rabbi began the entrance examination, he said, "I would like to ask you two questions."

In utter fear, the boy nodded his head in feigned agreement.

Rabbi Shkopf's face broke out in a warm smile. "When was the last time you had a hot meal, and when was the last time you slept in a warm bed?"

Preparing a fresh meal for the neophyte, Rabbi Shkopf showed him a comfortable bed on which he could rest.

"The Holocaust made me forget the *Gemara's* questions," the old man told Rabbi Weinberger. "Siberia wiped out all of the commentaries' questions. But never, as long as I live, will I forget Reb Shimon Shkopf's two questions."

❧

Sometimes scenarios leave greater impressions than lectures. The impact on youngsters, even toddlers, of seeing millions of people united, listening to their leader read the Torah, will live on in their minds forever. That is the greatest reward a parent can have. Perhaps the adults will indeed miss portions of the speech, but a more cogent lesson will be remembered. If you imbue your descendants with such memories, you are guaranteed that your life's goals and aspirations will be etched in their hearts for eternity.

Next time you think of sharing a trip to the ballpark or a movie with your kids, think about giving them a spiritual journey that will last a lifetime — and more. Let them have memories of seeing, and being greeted, even blessed, by a learned Torah scholar who could have been their grandfather. Let them see the way matzoh was baked in the old country — by hand — by devoted workers who tremble at the thought of leavened bread on Passover. Let them visit an institution of Torah study where hundreds of young scholars sit and learn Talmud. You'll not only have a wonderful time, but your kids will experience Judaism in a way that they will never forget.

PARSHAS HA'AZINU

➣ Humble Beginnings

*I*n this *parsha*, Moshe sang the song of *Ha'azinu* (Hearken), a hauntingly prophetic piece replete with predictions and admonitions. It extols the virtues of Israel, yet forewarns them of a perilous future if they disobey the Torah. As he finished the song, standing with his disciple Yehoshua, Moshe was prepared to transfer the mantle of leadership of the Jewish people. "Moshe came and spoke all the words of this song in the ears of the people, he and Hoshea the son of Nun" (*Deuteronomy* 32:44).

Moshe equated his own stature with that of his student Yehoshua in order to show the world his high regard for the future leader to whom Hashem had entrusted His people. Yet there is something strange. Yehoshua is not referred to by the regal name that Moshe had long since given him; rather, he is called Hoshea. Before the hazardous mission of the spies almost 40 years prior, Moshe added the Hebrew letter *yud* to Hoshea's name (see *Numbers* 13:16). The *yud* represents the name of Hashem and was a source of protection for Hoshea against the malicious intent of the slanderous spies. From that day, Hoshea was always referred to as Yehoshua.

Why, then, at the height of Yehoshua's career, on the day he is to take over the reins of power, does the Torah refer to him as Hoshea? Is the Torah surreptitiously diminishing his stature? However, isn't that exactly what the Torah would wish to avoid?

➤➤➤

On April 12, 1945, Vice President Harry S. Truman was summoned to the White House and shown to the sitting room of the First Lady, Eleanor Roosevelt.

Gently, she told him that President Roosevelt was dead.

After a few moments of stunned silence, Mr. Truman composed himself and asked, "Is there anything I can do for you, Mrs. Roosevelt?"

The First Lady shook her head. "Is there anything we can do for *you*?" she asked. "For you are the one who is in trouble now."

———※———

Perhaps Yehoshua's crowning moment was also meant to be quite sobering. He was made to realize that the force behind his greatness would no longer be with him. The man who had crowned him with the glory of God's name was joining the Creator, leaving Yehoshua alone and diminished. At that moment, he was just Hoshea. It was then up to Yehoshua to remember from whence his greatness came and rise to the challenge.

Often we bask in the spotlight of greatness and expect to remain aglow when the source stops radiating. Unfortunately, we are not made of phosphorous. The time comes when our light must shine from within ourselves. Indeed, from that moment on Hoshea shined as Yehoshua. Given the task, we will shine too.

V'ZOS HABRACHA

⁀ *Contributions & Commitments*

On Simchas Torah we read the last portion of the Torah in which Moshe blesses *Klal Yisrael.* Oddly enough, the first verse is not a blessing, but rather tells why we are worthy of blessing.

"Hashem came from Sinai after having appeared at Seir and at Paran...then with His right hand He presented the fiery Torah to them [Israel]" (*Deuteronomy* 33:2).

Our sages explain that God appeared at Seir and Paran, nations that rejected the Torah, because the Jews were not the first nation to have been offered the Torah. An angelic representative of Hashem visited his counterparts from all the world's nations. The *Midrash* tells us that when the angel approached Edom (Seir), it was asked, "Tell us, what does it say in the Torah?" The angel replied, "Thou shall not kill."

"If that is the case, the Torah is not for us," Edom sharply replied. "We live and die by the sword."

The angel then approached the Ishmaelites. This time the angel chose to declare the prohibition of adultery. Ishmael refused to accept such a writ.

The *Midrash* tells us about other nations as well. Each one, upon hearing a capital or moral law, flatly refused to accept the Torah.

Finally, the Jewish nation was approached. They replied with words that have been etched as the eternal battle cry of the Jew, "We will do, and we will listen." Of course, the rest is history. Jewish history.

The *Midrash*, beautiful as it may be, is in fact quite difficult to understand. Prohibitions against murder, adultery, and stealing were embedded in human civilization since the time of Noach. They are all crimes proscribed by the Seven Noahide Laws. Why,

⁀ 194 ⁀

then, when murder was packaged as part of Torah dids Edom refuse to accept it? What is the difference to Edom if murder is prohibited as a Noahide Law or as a Torah Law?

Why did Ishmael refuse the Torah on the basis of its moral restrictions? Wasn't adultery prohibited as part of their Noahide Law? Why are Torah commitments more threatening to the nations than their own Noahide obligations?

⟶⟵

A pig and a hen were *shmoozing* one evening in farmer Smith's barn when they heard Mrs. Smith declare, "My dear husband, tomorrow, is your birthday. I am going to fix you the most delicious breakfast you've ever had. I'm going fresh out to the barn in the morning and making us the most delicious ham and eggs you have ever tasted."

The animals froze in fear. "Again she's coming for eggs," cried the hen. "She is always taking my eggs!"

The pig turned to the hen in disgust. "Big talker you are. You're just making a contribution. I have to make a total commitment!"

⟶⟵

The nations of the world understood that the Torah is not a guidebook that dictates our actions. It is the moral cast that molds our very essence. The command, "do not murder," is not only a restriction against homicide, it defines our attitude toward human life. It even prohibits us from humiliating someone — an act considered by the Talmud as tantamount to murder. It forces restraints on our tempers; it molds our values as a nation.

The Torah's command "do not steal" is not only a prohibition against larceny, as it is in Noahide form. It enforces our value of every possession that is not our own. It prohibits us from carelessly waking a neighbor from sleep. It destroys the concept of "finders keepers, losers weepers." It creates an atmosphere of respect of not even treading on a neighbor's property without permission.

The nations had laws, but those laws were kept or broken as single conduct issues. Those laws controlled movement, not mission. Adhering to them took effort, but the effort was only a contribution. We were the only nation ready to transform our psyche, attitude, and essence. We made the total commitment.

ימים טובים

Holidays

ROSH HASHANA

➤ *Knock, Knock!*

*T*he repetitive nature of every-thing associated with *Rosh Hashana* is quite noteworthy. During the entire month of *Elul*, we blow the *shofar* at the end of *Shacharis* (morning prayer). It is almost the opposite of our approach to *matzah*. Not only is *matzah* prohibited to be eaten on the day that precedes the *seder*, many have a custom to abstain during the first fifteen days of the month of Nissan before Passover. In fact, others abstain from *matzah* for an entire month in joyous anticipation of the upcoming spiritual crunch. Anticipating *Rosh Hashana* seems quite different. Instead of creating excitement by *not* blowing the *shofar*, we seemingly diminish our level of expectation by becoming accustomed to it. Of course, we must prepare ourselves. But while there is a lot at stake on Judgment Day, wouldn't an extemporaneous and unrehearsed shofar blast send more of a shiver down the spine, and more forcefully evoke feelings of repentance, than a *shofar*-blowing ritual performed daily for thirty days prior? Why don't we worry that by the time *Rosh Hashana* arrives, the sound of the *shofar* may feel all-too-familiar?

Selichos services also prepare us for the great day. Sefardic Jews have the custom to recite these pre-dawn prayers for the entire month of *Elul*, while Ashkenazic Jews recite them for more than a week before *Rosh Hashana*. Would there not be a consideration that many Jews might lose enthusiasm from all these pre-holiday supplications?

In the *Selichos* service, we beseech the Almighty as if we were destitute. "Like beggars and paupers we knock on Your door. On Your door we knock, Merciful and Compassionate One" We knock — not once, but twice! Isn't once enough? Surely G-d can hear us the first time!!

My brother-in-law, Rabbi Simcha Lefkowitz of Congregation Toras Chaim in Hewlett, tells the following story:

A *meshulach* (a man who raises funds for charity) came on a sunny Sunday morning to a large home in the Five Towns of Long Island. Eagerly, the man rang the bell and simultaneously knocked on the door. A woman, quite displeased, swung open the ornate portal to her home and, knowing the man's intent, began to shout, "What do you want? I never met you in my life! How do you expect me to give charity to someone I have never seen? I'm sorry, but this is my policy and I just can't give to you!"

The *meshulach* was not perturbed. Slowly, he walked around the block, and 15 minutes later he was back at the same door. Again he rang the bell, and again the woman came out shouting, "I told you I never met you in my life! How do you expect me to give charity to someone I have never seen? Didn't I clearly explain my policy to you?"

The *meshulach* just smiled as he replied, "You are absolutely correct. However, you forgot one small thing. You know me already! After all, we met 15 minutes ago!"

During the weeks prior to *Rosh Hashana* we must be aware that we may have to knock a few times before we gain entrance through the big door. The shofar blasts, the recital of Chapter 27 of *Tehillim* (Psalms) — *L'Dovid Hashem Ori,* — twice daily to end our prayers, and the daily *selichos* are all summarized in the words we recite each day, "like beggars we knock . . . we knock on Your door."

We must realize that it is necessary to re-acquaint ourselves with the commitments and the great resolutions that we accepted upon ourselves one year ago. But we must knock more than once, so that ultimately we, too, can smile at the One standing at the door and ask for all our desires. After all, we were just there. And He knows us already!

YOM KIPPUR

✐ Call to Arms

*Y*om Kippur, the ultimate day of repentance, requires that the Jewish nation simultaneously pray, fast, and ask for forgiveness. The day begins with the somber, quiet, and melodious intonation of *Kol Nidrei* (all vows) and ends with the entire congregation shouting *Hashem hu HaElokim!* (God is the Almighty) seven times in succession. Yet this practice seems odd. At the time when our strength is waning we offer our greatest and loudest pleas. Shouldn't we begin the day with strong requests for forgiveness and save the subdued prayers for when our bodies are weak from hunger and our lips parched from lack of water?

❧

Rabbi Yehoshua Heshel Eichenstein, the Ziditchover Rebbe, tells the following story:

One Friday, a man entered the study of the Tchortkover Rebbe with a request that was once very common:

"My son was drafted into the army," the man began. "However, we have a way out. On Sunday, we are going to a doctor who will falsely declare him unfit for service. This way he will be spared certain misery, perhaps even death, in that terrible army. Rebbe," he said, "I need your blessing that he successfully evade the draft."

The Rebbe quietly told him that *Shabbos* was nearing and he could not concentrate on blessings. The man should return to him on that evening after his *tisch* (ceremonious *Chasidic* gathering).

The man did so. After most of the *chasidim* had left, the man repeated his request almost verbatim.

Again the Rebbe was non-committal. "Return to me after the morning service," he said.

Unperturbed, the man said that he would really like to resolve the matter before Sunday morning.

Shabbos morning, after services, the man approached the Rebbe again, and calmly repeated the predicament. "Sunday morning I am going to a doctor who will falsely declare my son unfit for military service," he said. "Please pray that we will successfully evade conscription." The Rebbe was not moved. Again, he deferred until the afternoon.

At the third *Shabbos* meal, the scene was repeated again, precisely the way it had the previous three times. "I understand that you are leaving Sunday morning. Come back to me late Saturday night," the Rebbe said. "By then I will have an answer for you."

By this time, his *chasidim's* curiosity was piqued, for they had never seen their Rebbe so reluctant to grant a blessing, especially when it was one that would save a Jewish soul from the frightful Polish army.

Saturday night, a large crowd gathered as the man approached with his request. Frustrated and disgruntled, the man once again repeated his story, almost verbatim, for the fifth time.

Immediately, the Rebbe sprung from his chair and began to shout, "What are you asking me? Why would one even try to evade the service of our wonderful country? How dare you ask me for a blessing of that sort? Your son would make a fine soldier for our country. I wish him the best of luck in the army!"

The man quickly scurried from the room and left town. The *chasidim* stood shocked and bewildered. Never had they heard such an uncharacteristic outcry from their Rebbe.

"I will explain," the Rebbe said. "That man was a fraud. He had no son, and if he did, he wanted him in the army. He was sent by the government to test our loyalty. Thank G-d we passed the test."

"But, Rebbe!" the *chasidim* cried, "how did you know?"

"Simple," the Rebbe explained. "I watched his level of intensity. From the moment he met me until tonight he had no increase in emotion or feeling of desperation with each request. The moment I heard his request tonight, and it contained no more passion or desperation than his first request on Friday afternoon, I knew he was a fraud."

We stand in prayer an entire day, and end with the *Ne'ilah* prayer, after nearly 24 hours of pleading. Finally, the true litmus test of our sincerity comes as the heavenly gates are being closed. As the sun begins to set, our pleas should intensify, and that crescendo assures our sincerity. It also should assure us a happy, healthy, and sweet new year.

Sukkos

➣ *Postscript to a Verdict*

*T*he verdict is in. The jury has decided. And no one has informed us of the outcome. Yet no one is sitting in torment. Nor are anyone's eyes glued to the television, or ears to the radio, trying to get information about what decision was rendered. No pundits are making predictions, and the defendants seem impervious to their fate. In fact, they are getting on with the next step in life: they are buying their four species and building their *sukkos*.

Of course, the verdict has been rendered worlds away by an impeccable Judge and an irreproachable Jury: The judgment of *Yom Kippur* has taken place in the courtroom of God Almighty, amidst His heavenly hosts.

But somehow things don't feel as tense as we might have expected as we await that crucial verdict which decides our health and welfare along with that of all those we love and cherish. Why not? Of course, we are all human and it's difficult to walk around in a state of uncertainty until next year's *Rosh Hashana* when we pinch ourselves and realize that we were judged favorably. Yet perhaps there is another reason for our confidence, a fundamental principle that we all must understand.

Immediately after *Yom Kippur,* we leave our homes and enter an unstable, rickety abode — the *sukkah.* Its walls are thin, and its shelter quite penetrable. The dwelling that heralds our harshest seasons, fall and winter, is open to all the elements. Why do we expose ourselves as such? If we must sit in a state of vulnerability, shouldn't it be in the warmth and sunshine of the summer?

➤➤

During Israel's War of Independence shells were being fired into the populated areas of Jerusalem. The

Mishkenot neighborhood where Rabbi Aryeh Levin, the *Tzadik* (pious man) of Jerusalem, lived was like a ghost town. The streets were completely deserted. But Reb Aryeh went out, as he had important things to do. His children, dismayed as they were, knew better than to try to stop the great man from any of his *mitzvah* missions.

One day, Reb Aryeh had heard that the remains of 40 Jewish people were lying in the morgue of the Bikur Cholim Hospital. The guards had fled due to the severe shelling, and now the bodies were exposed to animals and plunderers. He had decided that he had to find a proper watchman.

People who saw him walking through the streets shouted from their windows, "Rebbe, it is so dangerous! Please go back home to your shelter!"

Reb Aryeh looked up. "The Talmud says, 'those who are messengers of a *mitzvah* are not in harm's way,'" he said. "Every bullet has its address. If the Almighty wants to harm me, then the shell will hit me even if I am in the bunker."

Every year after *Yom Kippur* we also go out in the street. We sit outside as a declaration of confidence: we *know* that Hashem has looked favorably upon us. We don't have to shelter ourselves in secured mansions, surrounded by bodyguards. We can sit assuredly in the open and proudly wave our 'sword' — the *lulav* — as we proclaim with confidence that we know the verdict, even though no clerk has read it. Hashem has blessed us with another year of life and happiness!

SIMCHAS TORAH

✑ *Walking in Circles*

*W*e Jews don't waltz. We don't rock. And we don't roll. We dance. Our dance has more symbolism than the Rhumba, it has more tradition than the Charleston, and it definitely has more spirituality than the Cha-Cha. We walk around the *bimah* holding the Torah scrolls. Also in most synagogues the *Bimah* is moved and then we continue to dance in a large circle called the *hakafa*.

What is it about that circular motion that seems to define the culmination of the High Holy Days? In fact, the entire holiday of *Sukkos* is one of circles. We sit encircled in a *sukkah* and we parade around the synagogue in a circular fashion with our *lulav* and *esrog*. Then on the seventh day, *Hoshana Rabba,* we circle the *bimah* holding *aravos* (willow branches).

We not only dance in circles, we read in circles. Every *Simchas Torah* Jews gather in synagogues to finish one cycle of Torah reading. We complete the Torah, and then in true circular fashion we read *Braishis*, beginning the Torah all over again.

Shouldn't the New Year's symbolism be one of rocketing forward in a straight line, representing a spirit of forging ahead? Why do we, in our ecstasy, go to one place only to circle around and end up back at the same place?

❧

Rabbi Israel Baal Shem Tov, founder of *Chassidus,* once explicated a Talmudic contradiction: the Talmud in Tractate *Rosh Hashana* tells us that a man is judged every day — even every hour. Yet the same *daf* (page) tells us that man is judged every *Rosh Hashana*. The Baal Shem Tov asked, "How do we reconcile these seemingly contradictory passages? "

The Baal Shem Tov answered with the tale of Chaikel the water carrier. One day, the Baal Shem Tov asked Chaikel, "How are you Chaikel?"

Chaikel sadly replied, "My life is bitter and full of pressure. I have no more strength to lift these buckets and deal with all those customers. And furthermore, I can hardly earn a living."

Another time the Baal Shem Tov asked Chaikel, "How are you Chaikel?" Chaikel grinned from ear to ear.

"Thank God, I am wonderful," he shouted. "Imagine me, old Chaikel and I have the strength to *schlep* these heavy buckets. And, thank God, I'm so busy with customers I can't keep up with their requests! I couldn't be happier!"

The Baal Shem Tov turned to his students and explained. "Though we are judged each New Year on the total outcome of the year, every day is a new *Rosh Hashana* — some days are easy, and others are tough as nails. Today's emotions may be different from tomorrow's and tomorrow's different from today's. Each step of the way is a new challenge. And every day has a new perspective and a new judgment."

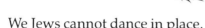

We Jews cannot dance in place. We must pass every corner of the synagogue and every member of the clapping crowd. We walk in a full circle with the understanding that there is no certain consistency to the moods and feelings that life will offer us. We must dance through the entire synagogue — sometimes stumbling on a rip in the carpet and other times gliding on smooth tiles. We pass the cracks in the walls, the wrinkles on the faces of the older folks and the candy-appled painted smiles of the little ones. And we dance around and around, knowing full well, that even though our journey may see smiles and frowns, and peaks and valleys, ultimately we will reach home again.

CHANUKAH

☙ Light up the Night

*T*he holiday of *Chanukah* is unique. Normally, Jewish ritual is observed privately, either in the home or the synagogue. Our Passover *seder* is celebrated as we sit comfortably behind closed doors. The *shofar* is blown within the synagogue. Even the *sukkah*, which is placed outdoors, lacks any mandate to be put on the front lawn: it can be discreetly ensconced in the backyard of one's home or behind a synagogue wall. Even the boisterous merriment of Purim does not call for revelry beyond the confines of the home or *shul*.

So why is it that only *Chanukah* exhorts us to display its main observance to the entire world? The *menorah* is *halachically* (legally) mandated to be displayed publicly. It should be lit in the doorways or windows of our homes, displayed proudly for all people to see. Why is there this public manifestation regarding this particular *mitzvah* more that any other? Is it not enough to celebrate this holiday intimately, in the home or synagogue, the same way that we celebrate every other observance?

The *Al HaNisim*, a prayer that is added for this holiday, contains a phrase that is similarly curious, about the *Maccabi* defeat of the Greeks. The Jews returned to the Holy Temple and they lit oil lamps in the courtyard of the Sanctuary. But what were those lights? The *Menorah* was lit inside the Temple. Why was this *menorah* lit in the courtyard?

Rabbi Shlomo Dovid Pfeiffer, a rebbe in our yeshiva, told me the following story:

Yaakov, a middle-aged scholar, was passing a home on a busy street when he was stopped by a stranger.

"Please, sir," the man said, "we are sitting *shiva* (in mourning) and need a *minyan* for the *kaddish*. Can you join us?"

The scholar gladly obliged. Upon entering the home, his eyes were transfixed by an odd scene. The four brothers who were sitting *shiva* did not look observant. Thin, black satin skull caps were perched upon their heads like birds about to fly away. The still life portrait of the room, however, was completely opposite. The *mezuzah* on the door was quite large, its wooden case well rubbed as if it had been kissed thousands of times. The large tomes of Talmud and *Shulchan Aruch* were well worn. Many of the bindings were ripped, and handwritten Hebrew notes lay stacked on top of the sacred volumes. An old pair of well-worn *tefillin* was unraveled in the corner of the room. Clearly, the living form of Judaism did not match the religious spirit of the deceased.

Yaakov turned to the oldest brother. He was a robust fellow whose partially unbuttoned shirt revealed a shiny *chai* chain buried in a thatch of graying hair. "I must ask you something," the scholar said. "If this was your father's home, it is evident that he was a very observant man. What happened to all of you?"

The four brothers looked at each other, and the youngest spoke. "Pop survived the Holocaust," he began. "In fact, Pop even claimed that during the war years he observed many *mitzvos* in secret. When he came to this country, he felt he had to do the same. He would hide in this room for hours before and after work. It was in this small room that he wore his *tefillin*. Here he prayed, and studied, and wrote. Frankly, we never saw exactly what he did, and soon enough we never cared."

⭆⭆

Perhaps the victory of *Chanukah* was more than a triumph of spirituality over hedonism. Maybe it was also a victory of open spirituality over closet observance. During the reign of the Greeks, Jews were hardly allowed to observe *mitzvos*, let alone study *Torah* openly. The Jews were forced to observe their sacred and beloved rituals in hiding. Our sages tell us that even the game of *dreidel* was played by children who had been studying *Torah* but replaced their texts with toys when Greek soldiers arrived. When victory was finally declared, our secret observances became open celebrations. A *Menorah* was even lit in the courtyard of the Holy Temple!

Chanukah is the holiday that reminds the Jew to be proud of his Jewish observance. As such, *Chanukah* is the holiday when children should see their parents light the *menorah*. After years of cowering and hiding, *Chanukah* is the time when Jews emerged and let their children know that they must openly display their *Yiddishkeit*. Even though there were times when God had to be served in hiding and under duress, when the proper moment arrives we are obligated light our candles publicly, openly, and brightly — for all humanity to see.

And so the candles that were lit in caves and in bunkers now shine proudly from doorways and picture windows for the whole world, and especially *our* world, to see. And despite any gusts of indifference, they continue to burn brightly as they light up the darkest nights.

PURIM

*W*hoever misses the Divine hand that touched the *Purim* story is not looking. And if he claims that he heard the *Megillah*, he probably was not listening. Imagine: Haman, the evil Prime Minister, draws lots and decides to annihilate the entire Jewish nation. Within 24 hours he has approval from the ruler of the not-so-free-world, King Achashveirosh.

Within days the plot is foiled, the Prime Minister is hanged, and his prime target is promoted to replace him! Pretty political. Pretty miraculous. And definitely Divine. Yet Hashem's name is not mentioned once in the *Megillah*. Why? Of course, the *Megillah* is replete with allusions. There are acronyms that spell the name of Hashem, and our sages explain that every time the word King is mentioned in the *Megillah*, it has a Divine reference. Why then does the last book of the Prophets, a Divinely inspired *Megillah*, have only veiled references to Heavenly intervention?

I once heard an auto industry fable. It was a sweltering August day when the Greenberg brothers entered the posh Dearborn, Michigan, offices of car maker, Henry Ford. "Mr. Ford," the eldest, Hyman Greenberg, announced, "we have a remarkable invention that will revolutionize the automobile industry."

Ford was skeptical, but his concern that they might offer it to the competition piqued his interest.

"We would like to demonstrate it to you in person," Greenberg continued.

After a little cajoling, they brought Mr. Ford outside and asked him to enter a black Edsel that was parked in front of the building.

Norman Greenberg, the middle brother, opened the door of the car. "Please step inside, Mr. Ford," he beckoned.

"What?" the tycoon shouted, "are you crazy? It must be 200 degrees in that car!"

"It is," Max, the youngest brother, smiled, "but sit down, Mr. Ford, and push the white button."

Intrigued, Ford pushed the button. All of a sudden a whoosh of freezing air started blowing from vents all around the car, and within seconds the automobile was not only comfortable, it was quite cool! "This is amazing!" Ford exclaimed. "How much do you want for the patent?"

Norman spoke up. "The price is $1 million." Then he paused. "And there is something else. We want the name 'Greenberg Brothers Air Conditioning' to be stamped right next to the Ford logo."

"Money is no problem," Ford retorted, "but no way will I have a Jew-name next to my Ford logo!"

They haggled back and forth for a while and finally settled on the price of $1.5 million dollars, but the name Greenberg would be omitted. However, the first names of the Greenberg brothers would be forever emblazoned upon the console of every Ford air conditioning system.

And that is why today, in every Ford car you will see those three names clearly printed on the air-conditioning control panel: HI NORM MAX.

❧

The *Megillah's* message accompanies us throughout our long exile: We may not see God's presence openly revealed in every circumstance. However, throughout persecution and deliverance, He is always there. On *Purim* His obvious intervention is undocumented, yet we know and feel it — and if we search, we will find it! So, too, in every instance we must seek His name, and recognize it. It may not be emblazoned on the bumper, it may be hidden on the console, but it is there. For Hashem is always leading. All we have to do is look.

PESACH

➤ Free at Heart

*T*he *Haggadah* begins with a preface. We point to the *matzah* and recite: "*ha lachma anya*. This is the poor bread that our fathers ate in the land of Egypt." The short paragraph ends with the hopeful words, "This year we are here; next year we will be in the land of Israel. This year we are restricted; next year we will be free."

Immediately after the *ha lachma anya*, the children ask the *mah nishtanah*, noting how different *Pesach* night is from all other nights. We respond to their questions by explaining that we were once slaves and Hashem redeemed us. We thereby give the impression to our children that *Pesach* night we celebrate our liberation. Yet, minutes earlier we had told our children that we are presently enslaved. It seems that our reply contradicts our previous declaration that "this year we are restricted; next year we will be free." What is the truth? Are we free or are we slaves? If we are free, then what is meant by the verses in *ha lachma anya*? And if we are not free, then what is the meaning of the *Seder*?

——※——

Two weeks after Anatoly (Natan) Sharansky was sent to Vladimir prison to serve a 13-year sentence, he was led to a meeting. To his shock, across the table sat his mother and brother Lenya. The conversation was never allowed to lead to anything substantial, and in fact it was quickly terminated when the guests were abruptly asked to leave. When the guard announced that time was up, Lenya pointed to the name boldly printed on Sharansky's prisoner's garb. "Tolya," he cried as the guard looked on, "you have your name on your outfit. I have it on mine, too!" With that, Lenya lifted his shirt to reveal a T-shirt with a picture of

Anatoly and the English words "Free Anatoly Sharansky!"

The guard quickly pushed the guests out of the room and snapped at Sharansky, "You will not see anyone for at least six months." Then he added sarcastically, "That's too bad."

"My sentence will end one day," Sharansky replied, "but what about yours? You are going to spend your whole life in jail"

~~✦~~

The *Haggadah* teaches us that one can be trapped in a country, in a civilization, or even in a jail — and still be free. The dreams and aspirations that were established with the liberation of body and soul thousands of years ago have become the symbolic unshackling of every mortal restraint. We may be behind Iron Curtains or iron bars, but we have the vision of freedom. We have the knowledge and experience that there is a better, more spiritual, more meaningful world outside the border of complacency. The guard who sneers behind his desk in Siberia is eternally subjugated while perceiving that he is free. We, on the other hand, have the vision for true freedom; and the aspiration for a better life, a better land, and a better existence; this keeps us free despite the chains of our mortality.

We may begin the *Seder* with the words, "now we are bound, next year we will be free," but those are only comments about physical freedom. They apply to the mortal bodies trapped in Auschwitz, in the Gulag, or in the depths of poverty and debt even in the most democratic country. But the dreams of true freedom and spiritual redemption were fulfilled more than 3,000 years ago near the banks of the Nile. And that emancipation of the Jewish People will never be subject to chains. That is the freedom that no one can take from us. That is the hope that we all can live and relive. That is the story of our emergence to freedom. It lives on forever. And anyone can relive it — anywhere, anytime. All you need is Torah vision and a dream.

SHAVUOS

⤳ *The Many Faces of Joseph*

*T*he *Talmud, Pesachim 68A*, tells of an interesting ritual performed by Rabbi Joseph. Each year, on the holiday of *Shavuos*, Rabbi Joseph announced, "Prepare a delectable calf for me. After all, if it were not for this special day, how many Josephs would there be in the marketplace?"

Simply stated, Rabbi Joseph felt that *Shavuos*, which commemorates the receiving of the Torah, elevated him from a common Joseph to the stature of the acclaimed Rabbi Joseph.

But what does he mean by "how many Josephs would there be in the marketplace?" Why use the plural expression, "how many Josephs"? Would it not suffice to say, "I would be like any Joseph in the market?"

⤳

Isaac Bashevis Singer tells the story of a man who returned from Vilna and said to his friend, "The Jews of Vilna are a remarkable people. I saw a Jew who studies all day long. I saw a Jew who spent all day scheming how to get rich. I saw a Jew who was waving the red flag and calling for a revolution. I saw a Jew who was loyal to his country. I saw a Jew running after his desires all day. And I saw a Jew who was ascetic and avoided temptation."

The other man said, "I don't know why you're so astonished. Vilna is a big city, and there are many Jews, all types."

"No," the first man said, "it was all the same Jew."

⤳

Rabbi Yaakov Yitzchak Ruderman, of blessed memory, the *Rosh Yeshiva* of Yeshiva Ner Israel in Baltimore, once explained that the *Torah* personality is constant and consistent in his every action, in his every mode of life. Unlike some who have one moral standard in the home, another in business, and yet another at leisure, the *Torah* personality demonstrates unwavering, consistent commitment in every aspect of living. Unfortunately, outside of *Torah* one Joseph may turn to many Josephs. There may be the Joseph who is honored for his charitable work, yet at home he may be an abusive and demanding Joseph — totally foreign to the Joseph who accepted an award at the podium hours earlier. There may be a Joseph who sways fervently in the synagogue, yet he cheats assiduously at business.

Rabbi Joseph celebrated because he found himself to be one unwavering person whose consistency in life was guided by one stabilizing factor — the *Torah*. "If not for this day," Rabbi Joseph said, "there would be many aspects to my life and much diversity in my character. My whims and fancies would guide my actions and I would eventually assume multiple characters. And there would be many Josephs in the marketplace."

On *Shavuos*, after receiving the *Torah* Rabbi Joseph could proudly say, as proud as the nation that received the *Torah* said, "We — or I — am one!"

TISHA B'AV

✎ A Kiss Missed

At every wedding we break a glass. It reminds us that there is no complete joy until Jerusalem will be rebuilt. After every Shabbos and holiday meal, before we recite *Birchat Hamazon*, (Grace after Meals) we recite the psalm of *Shir Hama'alos*. In it we talk about the return to Zion and only then will our mouths be filled with joy (*Tehillim* 126:2-4).

It seems that for serious Jews there is no complete joy even on the happiest occasion. Even the return to the Land of Israel and the re-establishment of a homeland there does not impede the mourning that *Tisha B'Av* commemorates. Why?

How is it that marriages, births, and even self-rule do not totally mitigate the pain of destruction. Why is the Jewish psyche so filled with the remembrance of sorrow. Is there never a time to move on?

During the years of World War II, Rabbi Shneur Kotler escaped to Palestine where he studied Torah uninterrupted. His father Rabbi Ahron Kotler, remained in Europe as *Rosh Yeshiva* of Kletzk while Reb Shneur stayed with his maternal grandfather Rabbi Isser Zalman Meltzer, one of the most venerable sages of his generation and *Rosh Yeshiva* of Yeshiva Eitz Chaim in Jerusalem.

Immersed in Torah study, Reb Shneur acquired the tools that enabled him to lead the Lakewood Yeshiva some twenty years later.

Reb Shneur became like a son to Reb Isser Zalman and his Rebbitzin Baila Hinda who cared for every one of his personal needs.

During that time Reb Ahron escaped to America and re-established the Kletzker Yeshiva as Beth Medrash Govoah in Lakewood, New Jersey. Even after the war ended, Reb Shneur did not join his family in the United States, but continued to study intensely. In 1947 his father decided that it was time for Reb Shneur to come to America.

It was an emotional departure from Reb Isser Zalman's home. The boat would be leaving in a few hours and the old taxi had pulled up near the door of the tiny apartment. Reb Isser Zalman and his Rebbitzen said their last good-byes. It may well have been the last time they were to see their beloved grandson. As Reb Shneur was about to enter the cab, Reb Isser Zalman bent down to kiss Reb Shneur but abruptly stopped. It seemed that something pulled him back. He stood erect, pursed his lips in pain, and said good-bye.

A student who observed the scene, could not contain himself. Immediately after the taxi left he presented his question to Reb Isser Zalman. "I don't understand," asked the student. "It seemed as if the Rebbe was about to hug and kiss his grandson good-bye, but suddenly stopped. What went wrong?"

Reb Isser Zalman nodded. "Of course I wanted to kiss him good-bye.

"But as I leaned forward I thought about the past ten years. How many grandchildren have no grandparents to kiss? How many grandparents have no grandchildren to kiss? They do not even have markers to visit. Thinking of them I felt selfish to kiss my own grandson, Reb Shneur, good-bye."

The sadness of *Tisha B'Av* lives on in every concerned Jew's heart until the memories of pain will be mended. Our joy is not complete with the recapturing of Jerusalem or even in the rebuilding of its walls. It is not totally fulfilled in the union of a young couple. Our prayers for the return to Zion encompass more. We want more than what we lost. We want consolation for every ruined Jewish community and its soul. We yearn for the spirituality that was destroyed. And we who believe in *T'chiyas HaMaisim* (revival of the deceased) understand that until the time that every grandchild can kiss his grandfather, our joy is incomplete.

And we yearn for the time that we can enter the holy city of Jerusalem in great joy with every loss that we have endured, mended. It will be a time when we can bend and kiss the rebuilt stones of our holy city with only tears of joy.

Biographical Data

Alter, Rabbi Yisrael of Gur (1895-1977) was the son of the last Gerrer Rebbe in Europe, Rabbi Avraham Mordechai Alter. He re-established the Gerrer *chasidus* in Israel and throughout the world after the decimation of Polish Jewry in World War II. He is also known as the *Bais Yisrael* after the commentary he wrote.

Alter, Rabbi Yitzchok Meir of Gur (1799-1866) founded the Gerrer *Chasidic* dynasty and author of the *Chidushei HaRim*. In addition to his *chassidic* leadership he was recognized as a foremost Talmudic scholar.

Auerbach, Rabbi Shlomo Zalman (1910-1995) was one of the foremost Torah scholars of our generation Dean of Yeshiva Kol Torah in Jerusalem, his *halachic* rulings guided thousands the world over.

Baal Shem Tov, Rabbi Yisrael (1698-1760) was the founder of *chasidus*. He lived primarily in Medzhibozh but often traveled all over Eastern Europe to spread the message of *chasidus*. He had many disciples who became *chasidic* leaders.

Berditchev, Rabbi Levi Yitzchak (1740-1809) was a student of the Mezhricher Magid and a widely revered *chasidic leader*. Author of *Kedushas Levi*, he is best known for his advocacy of all Jews.

Bunim, Irving (1903-1980) was an American Orthodox lay leader and teacher. Founder of the Young Israel movement, he played a prominent role in the World War II rescue efforts on behalf of *Va'ad Hatzalah*. His work on behalf of Torah Judaism in his day was unequaled.

Chofetz Chaim (1838-1933) *Rabbi Yisrael Meir HaKohen of Radin*, was known by the title of his premier work on the laws of speech. Author of numerous books on Jewish law, including the classic *Mishne B'rurah*, he was revered for his wisdom and piety.

Czernobel, Rabbi Mordechai Twerski of (1770-1820) was the author of *Likutei Torah*. A *chasidic* master he left eight sons, each a *tzaddik* in his own right.

Dubno Magid (1741-1804) Rabbi Yaakov Kranz was one of the most famous preachers of his time. His speeches were compiled into a book *Ohel Yaakov*.

Feinstein, Rabbi Moshe (1895-1986) was the Rosh Yeshiva of Mesivta Tiferes Yerushalayim in NYC and leading halachic authority of his day. He authored *Igros Moshe* and *Dibros Moshe* classic works of responsa and Talmudic analysis.

Finkel, Rabbi Nosson Zvi, (1849-1927) the *Alter* of Slobodka was the founder of the Slobodka Yeshiva, in Lithuania, and of the Chevron Yeshiva. He produced students who emerged as the rebuilders of Torah in the post-

Holocaust era.

Friedman, Rabbi David Moshe of Tchortkov (1827-1904) was known for his love of all Jews. After the death of his father in 1895 he settled in Tchortkov where he established his court. His talks were transcribed in Divrei David and Bais Yisroel.

Freifeld, Rabbi Shlomo (1923-1988) was known as a maser of bringing Jewish souls back to their roots. A student of rabbi Yitzchok Hutner, he was the founder and Rosh Yeshiva of Shor Yoshuv Institute in Far Rockaway until his untimely passing.

Halberstam, Rabbi Chaim (1793-1876), was a student of Rabbi Naftali of Ropshitz, with a reputation for compassion and charity that spread from Galicia across Europe, he is the forebear of the Bobov-Sanz dynasty and author of the *Divrei Chaim*.

Halberstam, Rabbi Yekusial Yehuda of Klausenberg (1904-1994) was the leader of the hasidic community of Klausenberg (Cluj), Romania. During the WW II he was interned in Nazi concentration camps where his wife and eleven children perished. After the liberation he rebuilt his life and established and nourished large communities both in the US and Israel.

Halstock, Rabbi Yechiel Meir of Ostrovtze, (1855-1920) was the son of a pious baker, and renowned for his self-deprivation and removal from worldly pleasure. He had hundreds of followers.

Horowitz, Rabbi Naftali (1760-1847), of the Polish town of Ropschitz, was born on the holiday of *Shavuos*. Considered one of the great *Chasidic* masters and teachers, his students included the *Divrei Chaim* of Sanz, the forebear of the Bobov dynasty.

Kagan, Rabbi Abba Shaul HaKohen (1936-1998), was the son of Rabbi Yehuda Leib Kagan and a dear student of Rabbi Ahron Kotler. Rabbi Kagan founded Kollel Bais Yitzchok of Pittsburgh Pa. where he served as Rosh Kollel until his passing in 1998.

Kagan, Rabbi Yisrael Meir HaCohen see **Chofetz Chaim.**

Kamenetzky, Rabbi Yaakov (1891-1986) was *Rav* of Tzitivyan, Lithuania, and Toronto, Canada. Appointed *Rosh Yeshiva* of Mesivta Torah Voda'ath in 1956 and a member of the *Moetzes Gedolei Torah*, (Council of Torah Sages), he was known for his brilliant Torah solutions and advice in a wide array of matters. He authored *Emes L'Yaakov*, an elucidation of the Torah and Talmud.

Kaplan, Rabbi Mendel (1913-1985) was a student of Rabbi Elchanan Wassermann of Baranovitch, Poland. In 1965 he was appointed a *Magid Shiur* at Talmudical Yeshiva of Philadelphia, where he was a *Rebbe* to hundreds of students until his death.

Kotler, Rabbi Yosef Chaim Shneur (1915-1982) was the sole son of Rav

Ahron, and grandson of Rav Isser Zalman Melzer. Reb Shneur became Rosh Yeshiva of Beth Medrash Govoah in Lakewood after the passing of his father in 1962. He authored *Noam Siach*.

Kranz, Rabbi Yaakov see Dubno *Magid*.

Levi Yitzchok, Rabbi of Berditchov (1740-1809) was a student of the Magid of Mezhritch, he authored the *Kedushas Levi* on the Torah. He is best known as a n advocate of Jews and an exemplary love for the simplest Jew.

Levin, Rabbi Aryeh (1885-1969) was revered by the entire population of Israel and the Diaspora. As voluntary chaplain to the leper hospital and prisoners of the British Mandate in Palestine, his saintly character earned him the admiration and love of thousands.

Lipkin, Rabbi Yisrael of Salant (1810-1883) founded the *mussar* movement and Rosh Yeshiva in Rameilles and the Kovno Kollel. Author of *Ohr Yisrael*.

Lopian, Rabbi Eliyahu (1876-1970) was a *Rosh Yeshiva* in Kelm, Poland and in Yeshivas Chayai Olam in London, England before becoming the *Mashgiach* of Yeshivas K'far Chasidim, near Haifa.

Melzer, Rabbi Isser Zalman (1870-1953) was the Chief Rabbi of Slutzk, Poland. Founder of the Yeshiva in Kletzk, Poland, in 1925 he was appointed to head the Eitz Chaim Yeshiva in Eretz Yisrael. Instrumental in the founding of a network of Torah-true day schools in Israel, he was a beloved teacher to thousands of students.

Morgenstern, Rabbi Menachem Mendel (1787-1859) the Kotzker Rebbe, a leading *Chasidic* figure in Poland. Known for his sharp wit and keen insight into human nature his acute philosophies awoke the hearts and souls of thousands of Jews.

Nachmanides (1194-1270) Rabbi Moshe ben Nachman of Gerona, Spain was a prolific author and brilliant scholar who defended Judaism in the debates at Barcelona. In addition to his masterful commentary on the Torah, he wrote on a large portion of the Talmud and on Jewish philosophy.

Rashi (1040-1105) Rabbi Shlomo Yitzchaki was the premier commentator on virtually every section of the Torah, Prophets, and Talmud. In addition to owning a winery in southern France, he headed one of the greatest Talmudic academies of his era.

Ruderman, Rabbi Yaakov Yitzchok (1900-1987) was a student of Slobodka Yeshiva and a colleague of Rabbi Yaakov Kamenetzky. In the early 1940s he founded *Yeshiva Ner Israel* in Baltimore, where he was the Rosh Yeshiva until his passing.

Sanz, Rabbi Chaim of, see **Halberstam, Rabbi Chaim of Sanz**

Sher, Rabbi (Yitzchak) Isaac (d.1952) was the son-in-law of the Alter of Slobodka and Rosh Yeshiva of Slobodka Yeshiva in Europe. He remained Rosh Yeshiva after it relocated to B'nai Berak, Israel.

Shkopf, Rabbi Shimon Yehuda HaKohen (1860-1940) was Rosh Yeshiva in Maltch and in Grodno, and was one of the foremost European Torah scholars in the period ending with World War II. His students included many luminaries who became prominent Roshei Yeshiva in America and Israel.

Shmuelevitz, Rabbi Chaim (1902-1978) was *Rosh Yeshiva* of the Mirrer Yeshiva in Jerusalem, where his brilliant *shiurim* (Talmudic discourses) and *shmuessin* (ethical talks) were renown.

Silver, Rabbi Eliezer (1881-1968) was a prominent figure in the emerging American Torah community. A powerful, witty, and brilliant leader, upon coming to America he was Rabbi of Harrisburg, Pennsylvania ending his career as Rabbi of Cincinnati, Ohio. He was a founder of the *Vaad Hatzalah* during World War II.

Sofer, Rabbi Moshe of Pressburg (1762-1839) was the leader of Hungarian Jewry during the emergence of the Reform movement which he battled fiercely. Rabbi Sofer authored numerous works on responsa, Chumash and Talmud. Many of his works are titled Chasam Sofer, a name by which he was better known.

Soleveitchik Rabbi Chaim (1853-1918) was the *Rosh Yeshiva* of Volozhin and Rabbi of Brisk. In addition to his brilliant approach to Talmudic law and reason, he was also known for his extreme piety and saintly nature.

Soleveitchik, Rabbi Yosef Dov (1820-1892) was Rosh Yeshiva in Volozhin and later the Rav of Slutzk and Brisk. Authored *Bais HaLevi* elucidation on the Torah and responsa.

Spector, Rabbi Isaac Elchanan (1817-1896) was the *Rav* of Kaunas, Lithuania and the foremost leader of European Jewry in the late 1800's. His responsa have become integral in formulating Jewish Law until this day.

Spira, Rabbi Yisroel (1892-1990) succeeded his father as Rebbe of Bluzhov in 1931. After suffering five years in Nazi concentration camps, and losing his wife, daughter and grandchild in the Holocaust, he settled in the United States and served as a member of the *Moetzes Gedolei Torah* (Council of Torah Sages).

Tchortkover Rebbe, see Friedman, Rabbi David Moshe

Sources

Boller, Paul F., *Presidential Anecdotes,* ©1981; *Congressional Anecdotes,* © 1991, Oxford University Press

Bunim, Amos, *A Fire in his Soul: Irving M. Bunim, The Man and His Impact on American Orthodox Jewry,* © 1989, Feldheim Publishers.

Fadiman, Clifton, *The Little, Brown Book of Anecdotes,* © 1985, Little, Brown & Co.

Greenwald, Yisroel, *Reb Mendel and His Wisdom: The Enduring Lessons Of The Legendary Rosh Yeshiva, Rabbi Mendel Kaplan,* © 1994, Mesorah Publications Ltd.

Himelstein, Shmuel, *Words of Wisdom, Words of Wit,* © 1993, Mesorah Publications Ltd.

Koppelman, Rabbi Dovid, *Glimpses of Greatness,* © 1994, Moznaim Publication Co.

Krohn, Rabbi Paysach J., *The Magid Series,* © 1987-1996, Mesorah Publications.

Raz, Simcha, *A Tzadik in Our Time The Life of Rabbi Aryeh Levin,* © 1976, Feldheim Publishers.

Rosenblum, Yonason, *Reb Yaakov: The Life and Times of HaGaon Rabbi Yaakov Kamenetzky,* © 1990, Mesorah Publications Ltd.

Sharansky, Natan (Anatoly), *Fear No Evil,* © 1988, Random House

Teller, Hanoch, *And From Jerusalem His Word: Stories and Insights of Rabbi Shlomo Zalman Auerbach,* © 1995, NYC Publishing Company.

Twerski, Rabbi Dr. Abraham J., *Not Just Stories,* © 1997, Shaar Press; *Generation to Generation,* © 1991, C.I.S. Publications

Weiss, Rabbi Yosef Weiss, *Visions of Greatness,* © 1997, C.I.S. Publications

The author expresses his thanks to the following individuals who have contributed to the weekly FaxHomily and in turn, this volume, with anecdotes, insightful comments, and constructive criticisms.

Howard Birnbaum, Judith Fein, The Goldman Family, Adam Parker Glick, Yaakov Hagler, Rabbi Heshy Hissiger, Rabbi Sholom Kamenetzky, Avrohom Chaim Knobel, Rabbi Yussie Leiber, Ilan and Tova Pacholder, Victor Raykin, Rabbi Yaakov Reisman, Rabbi Shimshon Sherer, Neil Wallin, Rabbi Moshe Weinberger, Professor Mark Weinstein, Howard Zuckerman, Rabbi Meir Zlotowitz